LOST PLACES

Other anthologies from Paradise Press:

Queer Haunts (2003; expanded edition 2013)
Oysters and Pearls (2010)
People Your Mother Warned You About (2011)
The Best of Gazebo (2012)
Eros at Large (2013)
Coming Clean (2014)
A Boxful of Ideas (2016)
We Want to Tell You How (2018)

LOST PLACES
An LGBT Anthology

Edited by Jeffrey Doorn

Paradise Press

First published in Great Britain in 2023 by
Paradise Press, BM 5700, London WC1N 3XX.
www.paradisepress.org.uk

Introduction and selection copyright © Jeffrey Doorn 2023.
The individual authors retain copyright of their works.

The moral right of the various contributors to be identified as the author of their work has been asserted by them in their acceptance of the Copyrights, Designs and Patents Act 1988.

All rights reserved. No part of this publication may be reproduced, stored in a retrieval system, or be transmitted, in any form or by any means, electronic, mechanical, photocopying, recording or otherwise, without the prior permission of the copyright owner.

A CIP catalogue record for this book
is available from the British Library.

ISBN 978-1-90-458594-7
10 9 8 7 6 5 4 3 2 1

Printed and bound by P2D Books Ltd, Westoning.

Cover design by Russell Wilson.

Designed and typeset by Ross Burgess.
Set in Garamond, with headings in Gill Sans.

Dedicated to
Jill Gardiner
1959–2023

Contents

Introduction		ix
Acknowledgements		xii
Meetings at Mike's	*Elizabeth J. Lister*	1
Hope Springs	*Peter Scott-Presland*	2
Public Conveniences	*John Dixon*	16
The Biograph Boys	*Jeffrey Doorn*	26
Two Poems	*Jill Gardiner*	29
Night Off		29
Dining Out		30
On Railton Road, a Queer Walking Tour		
	Ian Townson	31
Obituary: Chariots, Shoreditch	*Zekria Ibrahimi*	44
The Viking, Birmingham	*Leigh V. Twersky*	52
A gents' toilet condom machine, SW5		54
The Last Gold Star Lesbian	*V. G. Lee*	55
One-way Transaction	*Adrian Risdon*	64
Going Back	*David Downing*	67
Finding and Losing Lesbian Spaces in Brighton and Hove,		
and Beyond	*Jill Gardiner*	80
The Carved Red Lion – 2 Essex Road Islington, London		
circa 1980	*Gary McGhee*	98
Clapham Common Diary	*John Dixon*	101
Gay Galleries Gone	*Jeffrey Doorn*	106
Out and Down in London and Paris	*David Flybury*	115
Lost Places	*Stephanie Dickinson*	127
Authors' Biographies		128

Introduction

Nearly sixty years ago, the Beatles sang:

> *There are places I remember*
> *All my life, though some have changed*
> *Some forever not for better*
> *Some have gone and some remain.*

For LGBT+ people, the places we remember as significant in our lives helped shape who we are and how we relate to the world. This anthology recalls such places now lost, either through physical alteration, changed character, redevelopment or demolition. Some may remain but are no longer gay or gay-friendly.

It is important not only to recall the venues and facilities of the past, but also to record these markers of our history and heritage before they are completely forgotten. They form part of our legacy to younger and future generations who might not otherwise have any idea such places existed or what part they played in our development as individuals or communities.

In these pages are short stories, poems, reminiscence and researched reportage. Included are pubs, clubs, social and campaigning groups and organisations, cruising grounds, shops, cinemas, saunas, cafés and more. Locations range from Birmingham to Brighton and Hove, Hastings, Oxford, London and even Paris.

We begin with Beth Lister's celebration of Gay

Authors Workshop meetings hosted by the late Michael Harth, a founder member of the group who encouraged new writers, helping to build their confidence, and provided a friendly, sociable atmosphere in which to flourish.

Other types of meeting places include cottages (public lavatories) where casual sex might or might not occur and sheltered spots among the trees and shrubs of Clapham Common before the great storm of 1987 altered the once-familiar landscape. One writer laments the loss of Chariots Sauna in Shoreditch while another imagines a fantasy romance amid the raunchy goings-on in a notorious cinema widely known as the Bio-grope.

While certain landlords barred or threw out gay people, others provided a friendly welcome and space not only for drinking, cruising and possibly meeting a partner for the night or longer. In some cases they were the gathering place for friendships, political alliances and protest movements to form. In yet others, do-it-yourself discos provided a safe, relaxed zone to dance and romance, years before the commercial scene appeared. Several contributions recall the songs that got us dancing and now, like Proust's madeleine, immediately conjure up the scenes, the atmosphere and people on those long-ago nights.

Not that places we thought of as ours were always trouble-free. Sometimes the venue's possibly one gay night was invaded or attacked by drunk or simply homophobic straight men. Queer solidarity and mutual support at such times provided a real sense of community. Several writers recall the help and comfort given by their fellows, to the extent of offering a place to stay during periods of homelessness. We also follow a walk to the sites of the Brixton gay squats, where a unique form of communal living proved a life-enhancing experience.

To be sure, there are a great many lost LGBT+ places not recorded here. One can think of Blackpool's original Flamingo, dubbed Europe's biggest gay nightclub, sadly demolished in 2007. In London, there is the famous Black Cap in Camden Town, with its renowned drag acts, or the less well-known Father Redcap at Camberwell Green, which had an upstairs room for dancing in the 1970s, where DJ Tricky Dicky got his start; then it went straight, later briefly gay again, but now is an African bar & restaurant, de Nollywood.

The Campaign for Homosexual Equality ran a Friday evening disco, Liberties, at the Hanover Grand, off Regent Street in the mid to late 70s. By contrast, the first gay super-club, Bang, ran Monday nights at the Astoria, Charing Cross Road; it later became G-A-Y until the site was swept away for a Crossrail (Elizabeth Line) station.

You may know or remember other places around the country or beyond which have also disappeared, whether victims of property developers, austerity-induced cuts or replaced by apps like Grindr and other online platforms. Perhaps a future edition could be compiled before such memories fade.

In the meantime, as you turn the pages of this collection, whether with a sense of nostalgia, surprise, or even disbelief, enjoy these vignettes of LGBT+ life and times in venues lost but found again for your delectation, illumination and perhaps inspiration.

Jeffrey Doorn

Acknowledgements

The image on page 20, Public convenience, The Polygon, Clapham 1973, was reproduced by kind permission of London Borough of Lambeth, Archives Department, document reference 04476.

The photo of the biograph, page 28, is from the UK LGBT Archive.

The photo of Lambeth Town Hall, page 42, is from Wikimedia Commons.

Other images in 'Railton Road, A Queer Walking Tour' (pages 31–43) are from the Townson archive, Bishopsgate Institute.

The photo of the London Apprentice, page 78, is by Stephen Harris.

The images on pages 112–114 are from postcards issued by Adonis Art or St Jude's.

We have made every effort to trace copyright ownership of illustrations; we apologise for any omissions.

Meetings at Mike's
Elizabeth J. Lister

Easy on the train to Euston, happy on to Homerton
Wine from the corner store;
Remember the roads, between trees in the park.
To your door.
Culinary evidence on your window sills,
Writer and author not your only skills.
Lover Lawrence busy with kettle on the boil
Teas for all or coffee as we unpack our spoil,
Tableful of goodies.

Oh, the happy meetings! Such acceptance there!
Reading out our writings, you sitting in your chair
Words and wine and laughing and eating up the food
So good!
Thoughtful on the tube to Euston, sleeping on the train to Stoke.
A Gay Author.

Hope Springs
Peter Scott-Presland

If you come into Oxford by coach, you will sweep down Headington Hill, through the tree-lined cut and under the footbridge which in 1972 linked the two parts of scoundrelly Robert Maxwell's Pergamon Press empire. The road flattens as you come to the nondescript St Clements, and then a roundabout ('The Plain') and Magdalen Bridge. Magdalen without an 'e' on the end – 'e's are for lesser mortals in Cambridge. Get off the coach opposite Queen's College, and walk back over the Bridge, the Cherwell now flowing from left to right. At the roundabout take the third exit – St Clements being the first – and you're in Iffley Road; immediately on the right is The Cape of Good Hope.

It's vaguely triangular. Google says of it 'British/European community gastropub with funky fabrics and light fittings, music and pub quizzes.' Step back in time fifty years, and it was a rough Irish pub, full of workmen in overalls and boots drinking quantities of Guinness just after a day's work. There were few tables – clients drank standing up. And it had that air of contemplative quiet which you used to get in pubs before they had televisions and fruit machines. There was a bar billiards table – you don't see many of them nowadays.

It could have done with a lick of paint, inside and out; as indeed could some of the customers. Some Irish pubs scream 'cliché', and The Cape did too. But the cliché was that of an Irish pub in Ireland – steady, sober drinking, earnest low voices discussing Joyce and jockeys. The landlord's name was Pat – well, it would be, wouldn't it? He was a tall man, so much so that when he leant on the bar he leant over it too, almost to your side. I remember a massive head furrowed with perpetual worry at some philosophic conundrum. Whatever it was, he was resigned to not solving it, for he was soft-spoken and stoical. Like the pub itself, he had seen better days. Later I discovered he had been a boxer.

This first visit to The Cape, sometime in the summer of 1972, I had a mission. I had put an advertisement in *Daily Information*, a Crown-size double-sided sheet which crammed everything you could want to know about the city's activities higgledy-piggledy across six columns. The publisher, John, used to cycle round Oxford with the paper origami'd into a tricorn, crying, '*Daily Information*! *Daily Information*! Read it as a newspaper, wear it as a hat!' *D.I.* as it was known, was the only possible outlet – both the *Oxford Mail* and the *Oxford Times* had turned down ads from the Campaign for Homosexual Equality.

'Want to start a gay group? Tired of nowhere to go?' asked the little box ad. – or words to that effect; I think there must have been something too about campaigning. It invited interested parties to a pub on the Botley Road, in Osney, the unfashionable side of town. I think it was then called the Marlborough Arms, although what is now the Osney Arms looks remarkably like it. Perhaps there was a name change. About twenty people turned up, and what was startling was the cross-section of Town and Gown – very unusual at the time.

CHE had two separate groups, one for the City and one for the University, each largely invisible. The City group I only discovered forty-five years later, researching CHE history for a book. The organiser of the Town Group was an elderly man called Leslie Jolly, who didn't want his name mentioned anywhere, not even on internal newsletters, and charmingly admitted his own deficiencies of courage and energy. This was essentially a social group.

The university group was run by a Dr Robin Robbins in Baliol College, whose wife Anna was having an affair with my flatmate John. She delighted in trying to shock people and embarrass John by loudly discussing the unusual shape of his penis. Robin always struck me as slightly sinister; with his steel-framed glasses he bore an unfortunate resemblance to some Nazi scientist in a war movie. He was very quiet, spoke out of the corner of his mouth, but, I'm told by members of the group, was very sweet and welcoming. Anna used to bang on about his penis too, and how large it was. His bosom chum was Andrew Watt, an extrovert undergraduate at Exeter College with a voice like a camp foghorn. An inveterate cottager, he had a passion for biting with his tombstone teeth, with the result that you could usually tell who had been to bed with Andrew by the hickeys on his neck. I was very fond of Andrew, who was bouncy, friendly, had very attractive marble-white skin, and was one of the few CHE members keen on sticking his neck out of the University shell. Others contented themselves with going to weekly socials with copious sherry organised by Christopher Strachey, nephew of Lytton, a computer programming pioneer and the perfect host.

By contrast, I remember from the Osney meeting Simon Martin, a Labour councillor and scrap dealer; to go to bed with him you had to clamber over the most amazing junk in his chock-full house – I had to negotiate an enormous figurehead and a stuffed bear once. Alex Smart-Gardener was an ex-ship's steward in his fifties, with a corset and a most unconvincing wig, which he swore blind was his own hair. He was in hospitality now, and became 'our hospitality', as you will see. Peter Watson, bald and sly, was some sort of businessman. The nature of his business was a bit shady, and he used to disappear for months at a time at Her Majesty's Pleasure. Rumour was that it was something to do with lead on church roofs, but I always thought that was rather too physical for Peter, who was large and looked distinctly unhealthy. From the university there was the aforementioned Andrew Watt, and Richard Krupp, another gay foghorn but with a New York accent. Jamie Gough, tall and gangling like a baby-faced Hugh Grant with glasses; Nigel Pinn, author of one of the first 'gay plays', *And What About Me?*, which I directed at the Oxford Playhouse that summer.

We all agreed 'A Plague on Both Your Houses' as far as being a CHE or a GLF group was concerned. Not CHE, for the reasons already stated, not GLF, because we had been subjected to a hectoring manifestation by some GLF people at a disco in Reading University. These men went around the innocent boppers saying that that they couldn't possibly be Gay unless they (a) came out to everyone and (b) gave up their male privilege by wearing radical drag and makeup. This was too much for some, especially those who had recently come out; while their slap, which made them look like pandas on acid, was hardly an enticing example. So, partly on aesthetic grounds, we became the Oxford Gay Action Group (OGAG).

The meeting was also very clear that Oxford needed two things: firstly a Gay Switchboard on the lines of the New York one – there were none at all in the UK at the time, at least not as such. Although London FRIEND had had a telephone service allied to personal counselling since October '72. That is a separate story, really, but Oxford Gay Switchboard opened in September 1973, six months before the London Switchboard and the first in the country.

The second thing that Gay Oxford needed was a regular disco, both in its own right and as a fundraiser to pay for the Switchboard, publicity and other campaigning. There was no disco nearer than London, Bristol or Birmingham; while the pub scene consisted of little enclaves in the Red Lion, by the bus station, and the Kings Arms, near Hertford College. The KA scene was a little series of student cliques, circles of friends difficult to penetrate. The Red Lion was generally thought to be the Town's real gay pub.

The first time I went there, in 1971, a year before Osney, I was scared witless of what nameless horrors I might find, not to mention the chance of being spotted going into it. Opposite the pub was a cinema, the ABC, and one cold Sunday evening in November I lurked in its entrance screwing my courage to the sticking place. Every time I was just about fired up and halfway across the road, I'd see someone walking along the outside of the pub and veer back into the safety of my doorway. I pretended to be studying the stills on display; the film was *One Million Years BC*, with Raquel Welsh and John Richardson. I realise now this must have been the late-night Saturday offering, because the flick was already several years old.

Once the coast seemed clear, I took a deep breath and headed back towards the Saloon Bar – I must have assumed that the homosexuals would be posh and want carpets on their floors. But no, another person would come round the corner, so back to the lobby cards it was. Then I realised I was paying much more attention to the bearded butchness of John Richardson than the shapely Miss W, and blushed furiously. Surely someone must notice. Surely I was Obvious.

Finally, at 10.25 five minutes before closing time, I thought, 'It's now or never,' and flew in through the entrance into a rather quiet bar. I looked around for the homosexuals. It was so disappointing. Everyone looked exactly the same. It was impossible to tell who was who. I had a glass of Barley Wine to cover my confusion, then exited without speaking to anyone, in disarray. Later, at the Osney Meeting, I recognised Alex Smart-Gardner; he had been ensconced at the end of the saloon bar. By this time I had a student clique of my own at the King's Arms.

Oxford Gay Action group did a whole load of things outside of the Kings Arms, from going on Trade Union demos against the effects of Ted Heath's Industrial Relations Act, to a Pride Punt which invaded the male nudist enclave of Parson's Pleasure. But let's stick to the

Cape of Good Hope and the OGAG discos. Pat charged us the sum of £2 per week for the hire of the room every Friday; today that would be worth £25, still pretty cheap. But there was nothing else going on in the pub and he was glad of any revenue.

The room was the shape of a wedge of brie – the pub was on the junction of the Iffley and Cowley Roads. If you imagine the brie pointing towards you, the entrance was on the right hand side at the far end, up a narrow flight of stairs. It was bog-standard Brewery décor – red lino, beige walls, a brown dado rail. The brewery was Mitchells and Butlers, from which I developed a taste for a pint of mild and blackcurrant, a drink impossible to get nowadays.

The first thing needed to run a disco was a DJ with a mobile sound system – there was nothing in the pub itself. I'm not sure where Rob came from, but he was the real deal, and looked the part. Shoulder-length auburn hair, plum-coloured or turquoise crushed velvet Loon pants, beads, and a cheesecloth shirt opened nigh to the waist exposing downy chest hair. He wore mascara and blue eye shadow above chiselled cheeks – and he was straight. The most beautiful undergraduates failed to dent his heterosexuality; even Andrew Wyatt, who could open any pair of male legs as easily as a sardine tin, drew a blank. Despite this, I doggedly helped him down the stairs with his boxes of records at the end of every Friday evening and once even got a lift from him to Headington when he was going on to play a late-night gig at RAF Benson. My hopes rose when I realised taking me home was a bit out of his way, but were dashed again when he stopped outside the flat to let me off and offered to sell me half an ounce of black for twenty quid. This was not what I had hoped for, but I took half of it, and very good it was too.

There are some songs I can never hear without remembering that room and that disco. So much Bowie – 'Changes', 'Oh You Pretty Things' (that was us), 'Life on Mars', and of course 'Queen Bitch':

> *You're so swishy in your satin and tat,*
> *In you frock coat and bipperty-bopperty hat*

was a fashion statement we all aspired to, while we all thought,

> *It could have been me*
> *It could have been me*
> *Why didn't I say? Why didn't I say?*

about someone or other (Oh Rob! I sighed). 'Suffragette City' and 'Jean Genie' joined our Bowie playlist on the floor. In our minds Bowie was inseparable from Lou Reed, with whom he was hand in glove, and elsewhere. We loved almost everything on *Transformer*. 'Vicious' ('You hit me with a flower') was eminently danceable-to, closely followed by 'Walk on the Wild Side', with its nonchalant celebration of trans-transgression. How we strutted, wishing we were so daring! While, from the start of 1973, the disco always closed with 'Goodnight, Ladies'. It wasn't exactly a dance tune, but the great advantage of the Cape of Good Hope upstairs was that the room was large enough to allow plenty of space to spread your terpsichorean self. So when tracks were symphonic (this was the era of the concept album), dancing could be balletic. Pink Floyd gave us 'Time' and Led Zeppelin, 'Stairway to Heaven'. But nothing in the leaping, prancing, twirling, on-your-knees department could compete with 'The Lemon Song':

Squeeze me, babe, till the juice runs down my leg.

Boy, how we loved to milk that one.

At the risk of being a name-dropper, I'll mention a few of the many people who became prominent in the LGBT movement later, who flounced on the floor of the OGAG disco and I hope derived some confidence as well as some fun from it: Jonathan Walters went on to be the first paid worker of the Joint Council for Gay Teenagers, and brought to fruition the first authentic voice of gay youth for publication (*Breaking the Silence*). Andy Lippmann, of unearthly pallid beauty and blind as a bat, shocked some with his early espousal of leather; he went on to direct the brilliantly satiric *Watch Out, There's a Queer About* about vicious police methods against gays. It was all the more effective for being bang on the button in terms of factual accuracy. Roger Juer was something big in Planning at Oxford City Council, and remains a fiery but camp queer activist to this day. Roland Jeffries, unusually bearded for the time, set many hearts aflutter, before going off to be FRIEND's first paid worker. Graham McKerrow, later founder editor of *Capital Gay*, came along as a shy coltish 17-year-old, under the wing of an enormous lesbian called Louie.

We started with maybe thirty people, some from ads but mostly friends of friends. Word spread quickly in the village that was queer Oxford. Soon we were able to buy phone equipment and pay the rent on a back room of a radical bookshop, Uhuru, for our pioneer Switchboard.[1] In six months we had more money than we knew what to do with, and financed conferences, sent delegates over the country, and supported queer arts.

I was involved with OGAG for something like two years, and only once was there a shadow over the disco. In the winter of 1973/74 there were threats against the Gay Switchboard which made it pretty clear that the bullies knew where we met and where we danced too; it was a time when Fascist activity was reported in the car plants at Cowley. The Cape had a couple of bricks through the window on a Saturday, whether as a warning or because they'd got the wrong night we never knew.

By this time the regulars had got used to us. When we started there was no bar upstairs, but it became increasingly clear that it was not practical to have up to 100 people up and down the stairs with pints in their hands. At first when we descended to the saloon to order there were nudges and sniggers, though no overtly hostile reactions. After a few weeks OGAG regulars got to know pub regulars, we spilled into the Public Bar with the weight of numbers, and started to acknowledge each other. A few more weeks, and you could hear some Irish

---

[1] For a fictional representation of the Oxford Switchboard at this time, see my play, *Nothing Personal*, on YouTube.

accents on the disco floor, and queeny voices over the bar billiards.

So when the bricks came through the windows of the pub, the Irish regulars took it as a personal insult. With great resource, Pat recruited volunteer escorts from the Public. We upstairs took lists of people who felt that they might feel threatened going home. If you were in college, it was essentially a matter of getting across Magdalen Bridge to the comparative safety of the High Street and the Colleges. For others the goal was one of the numerous bus stops. When the disco turned out, escorts paired up with disco-goers and went off in their respective directions. The sight of these beefy labourers, many of whom worked on building sites, flanking our queens in seersucker shirts and bell-bottoms, was enough to keep any threat at bay. At the end of the 'airlift', as it was nicknamed, Andrew Wyatt was a bit disappointed. He'd done quite well for trade out of it.

Only one other highlight: some time in 1974 we needed to do a fundraiser, I think for a conference. We decided a cabaret was the answer, and threw together some dozen items, with piano provided by David Harrod, with whom I went on to write musicals. Several alumni of OUDS,[2] not themselves gay, volunteered their services, the most outstanding being Christina Matthews who had great success later in West End musicals, most notably in *Mr Cinders* and *42nd Street*. I can still see her astride a bentwood chair belting out Sally Bowles' 'Don't Tell Mama' – this was before the film came out.

---

[2] Oxford University Dramatic Society

I teamed up with Nigel Pinn to write some new sketches and songs – one of my first attempts in the field. When Nigel teetered on stage in very high heels and a blonde wig, leered at the audience and intoned throatily:

> *Falling in love again, isn't it obscene?*
> *At seventy I'm still queen*
> *I can't help it…*
>
> *Men cluster to me, all races and all lands*
> *The fees that are due me*
> *Keep me in monkey glands …'*

The roar went on for several minutes, and he had to repeat the whole thing, twice.

We were absolutely starved of anything resembling gay entertainment or positive images. The show, which cost £1.50 to get into, ran for three nights, and by the last night not only did we have far more people in the audience than the 120 the space was licensed for, the queue to get in ran right round the pub. People were offering £10 to get in… £20… some had come from as far away as Stratford and Warwick, so desperate were they for some form of contact. I could have had sex ten times over that evening in exchange for the magic die stamp on the wrist, but I was honest – or maybe prudish.

Yes, prudish. One of the results of the way I came out was that I got into gay politics before I got into gay sex. An upbringing which never acknowledged anything personal had left me with a profound sense of my own unattractiveness. Seeing photos of the period now, I realise I was quite a looker, a slim and lithe Adonis in specs. More than one person has since told me that they fancied me something rotten, but didn't dare approach because I was always organising something; while I was always organising something as a shield from what I thought would be either rejection or certain sexual disaster. Not that there weren't some memorable one-night stands, in which I sampled the gay tasting menu over a number of months, and learnt a few lessons in the process.

Come June 1974, it was time to leave Oxford. I'd strung out my sojourn for six years, and couldn't milk another grant out of the DoE. There were few celebrations; it was in truth a huge wrench after six years living in the most beautiful, most infuriating city in England. I was however on my way to a brilliant job as the Administrator of the Birmingham Arts Laboratory – a job I had blagged my way into by lying through my teeth. I was way outside my competence, as any of the interviewers would have known had they bothered to ask me any questions about Contemporary Art.

I promised to go back to Oxford, of course, and did eventually. I found that OGAG had wilted and CHE thrived under Roger Juer. There were new weekly commercial discos in Oxpens, by the cattle market, and there was shortly to be a bona fide gay pub, The Jolly Farmers. Pat was gone from the Cape, the Friday discos had ended and all those university friends I'd known had dispersed their separate ways to infect the body politic with a bit of radicalism. Of the town, Simon Martin remained a

Labour Councillor and Alex still propped up the bar in the Kings Arms. Peter Watson was probably detained somewhere.

Our moment, our Cape of Good Hope moment, had passed.

Public Conveniences
John Dixon

The first term. The first year of secondary school. The playground. An older boy approaches a group of us First Years. What does he want? A fag – that is a cigarette – or an errand carried out? Is he a teacher's snout, come to suss out the new intake? An erstwhile sub-prefect who wants to get the low-down and run off and tell a master? No. He wants to pass on a dirty joke.

In those days there was no sex education at school or home; you learned from playground jokes, smut passed on surreptitiously. And you laughed whether you understood the joke or not. Indeed, if you didn't laugh, you'd be bypassed when the next joke did the rounds. You were expected to pass on the joke (even if you didn't 'get it' or couldn't remember it properly and were likely to fluff it in the telling).

I was hopeless. I'd had a sheltered upbringing, and was a bit slow on the uptake. One joke, that took years to filter through, was … Question – Why is a public lavatory a high-class place? Answer – Because that's where all the big knobs hang out.

At that tender age I thought big knobs were the leaders of society, venerable gentlemen, from the highest rungs, of noble descent, leading exemplary and blameless lives, and setting an example to us all.

There was no reason to know about public lavatories. I don't think I was aware of toilets as entities separate from my home or the houses of relatives and friends. There were toilets at primary school, of course, in the cinema and perhaps in a big department store, but these were for the students of that school, the spectators at the cinema, the customers in the department store, etc. They were not located in public and just for – anyone.

When I was seven my parents moved out of London to Portsmouth – not the island itself, but the lower slopes of the hill that overlooks the city – and I first came conscious of the existence of toilets. First as overheard parental talk. My mother had made friends with a close neighbour, whose husband worked for the Portsmouth Corporation. He went round in a van collecting the pennies from all the public lavatories. My father, ever eager to belittle, made merry, questioning whether the pennies were also collected from the Ladies Toilets, wondering if any money went missing and how come Mother's friend had so many new clothes. This was just background chatter.

There were a few shops near us, but less than a mile away was a far larger shopping centre, Cosham. The main road there had a Co-op, a Woolworths, a Marks and Spencer's and two cinemas. Somewhat away from the centre was a public library. I was a regular visitor, initially hooked on the series, *The Famous Five*, *The Secret Seven*, *Jennings*, *William*, even *Billy Bunter*, but never *Biggles*. The library was situated on a large triangle, almost an extended traffic island. Next to the library was the Red Lion Pub, and a meeting hall. Along the sides of the triangle were houses. And at the flattened-off apex were public toilets.

This was also the end of the route for trolley buses. They were unable to go up the hill and lined up outside the toilets. I loved watching the trolleybuses arrive and the long pole hitched to the side of the bus used to disengage the poles connecting to the overhead wires. When the bus was due to leave, the overhead connections were re-engaged and the bus moved quietly off. I spent hours watching this process and would time how long it took from the arrival of each bus to the departure, and compare the break between work shifts to the breaks we had at school between lessons.

No doubt the drivers and conductors used the toilets and maybe also popped into the Red Lion. I occasionally used the toilets as there were none in the library. They were palatial, tiled and spotlessly clean. I was scared I might bump into the husband of Mother's friend.

Thirty years later, and somewhat worldly-wiser, in SW4, I found a déjà vu situation. At the end of my road is an area called the Polygon. It is situated at the corner of the Common, just behind Holy Trinity Church, the anti-slave-trade church of the Clapham Sect. It is enclosed by roads, and contains a few houses, shops and has that same combination of public buildings – public transport, public library, public house and public toilets. This time they are strung out, some within the Polygon, some along the roads that form the Polygon. All of them are separate buildings and occupy a separate space.

The area given over to the bus terminus is the largest used part of the Polygon. Old photos are available of horse-drawn buses, early motor buses with open tops and open spiral stairs at the back. Very much the site of the original Clapham Omnibus. There is still a horse trough. Currently the area is an open-air terminus for several bus routes.

The pubs, three of them, are The Sun, The Rose and Crown, and The Prince of Wales. The Rose and Crown is in the Polygon, the other two face it from each adjacent road.

The Library is also on an adjacent road, facing inwards to the Polygon. It is on two floors, and has a terracotta façade. The date of construction, 1889, is carved in the upper stonework.

Within easy reach of all of these three public facilities, centrally placed, isolated and rather incongruous is (was) a public toilet. In true cottage style, above ground, no steps, one storey, two halves, gentlemen and ladies. A steep tiled roof gave a toy-town, pixie hut effect. Railings enclosed small trees and shrubs. There was a metal grill at the entrance, and opaque, wire-reinforced glass windows. Inside was tiled, with two cubicles, three urinals and one wash-basin. It was regularly cleaned, but had no resident attendant. I can't remember the exact opening hours. After dark with the lights on and shadows projected it looked quite cute.

As I lived not 200 yards away there was little reason for me to use it. But I did, if not for its intended function. The toilet was on the doorstep, but not too close for comfort. It became an outward and return drop-by on the circuit of other loos and trolling grounds in the area.

It was also overlooked by several adjacent buildings. The library itself had no toilet facilities. I would regularly pop from reading a book to checking out the toilets. The

library had one other advantage. It was on two floors. The books were on the ground floor. The upper floor I suspect at one time might have been used for a reference section, meeting room, staff rest room, or even live-in janitor. Only occasionally in my time was the upper floor open for public access – an overspill during redecorations, or to house a special exhibition. The stairs, which overlooked the toilets, were tucked just inside the main entrance of the library. You could come and go without being challenged at the book issue desk. I was able to sit at the wide window ledge, overlook the toilets and see the comings and goings. Many a time I would dash out to check a newcomer. Equally I might see someone I'd recently met (and who'd promised to phone me) going in and quickly coming with a pick-up, whom I'd dearly have loved to have got for myself.

There were regular users. Local residents, nodding-acquaintance-only neighbours. The toilets were equidistant between the Wandsworth Road and Clapham High

Street, so were the object of more than one transport pincer movement. They were used by library members, pub goers, and of course, bus drivers and conductors. It was always a quickie with uniformed transport staff.

Then the area was afflicted by the worst blight conceivable, the weasel word, Regeneration. A row of nearby council offices was emptied out, for a short time given over to private offices, then inevitably revamped to flats. One by one the shops in and around the Polygon changed hands and function. The much-loved betting shop became a restaurant. Many of the other shops became estate agents. The library was relocated to the High Street, and the old library became a theatre, Omnibus, after the Clapham Omnibus. The bus terminus was redesigned, and the horse trough side-lined. An area once used for bottle banks became a patch for bee-loving wild flowers. One of the pubs, where you could once take your dog and sit in the gardens, now became a hiving pub for twenty-somethings, with overspill into the road and minicab drivers touting outside. All the facilities were taking on new roles.

But not the toilets. They didn't feature in any of the plans and models on show. As ever The Great Unspoken. Other toilets in the locality had succumbed. The toilet at Voltaire Road, which served the Clapham North Tube and rail station had closed some time ago, and the triangle it had been located on was paved over. The only remnant of its existence was a green pipe, about thirty feet high, of the sort often used for 'exhaust' from underground rivers.

The loo alongside Clapham Common Station – again on a triangular stretch, containing a row of bus stops, the tube and the toilets – was closed. Which was sad as it was busy and pleasant inside and as you stood waiting there was a skylight effect. The ceiling, made of opaque glass tiles, was set into the pavement. You could blurrily see the underside of shoes, and sometimes reckon if someone walking above you would come down the loo and stand next to you. This facility was sold off and converted into an underground wine bar. There is a large jokey notice outside – WC – which, of course, stands for **W**ine and **C**harcuterie Don't forget this is Clapham, pronounced Cla'h'm: the P is silent as in swimming.

Was the loo at the Polygon going to be dragged down to this yuppy level of joke consumerism? I had a suspicion, short of a conspiracy theory, that the loo was doomed. It was closed, and left to become derelict, condemned without consultation. Like publicly-owned industries and services, run down, made too expensive for repair. Profit-making criteria were applied to public service provision, plus a few scare-mongering hints of supposed sewage problems, posing a hygiene hazard.

The railings were removed, then the garden surround and shrubs. The whole area had a work in progress feel. And the toilets acquired a To Let notice.

There was some talk of it becoming an art gallery, part of a cultural hub, to tie in with the neighbouring Omnibus Theatre. A pedestrian crossing, leading from the Polygon to the rear of Holy Trinity Church, was opened, and remains perhaps the only worthwhile change in the whole Regeneration. A low wall was erected to cordon off the road. It also served as a park bench. Some spindly trees appeared.

There were no takers for the letting. In June 2017 consultants were brought in to hasten the letting. Their advert reads –

The Property is located at the northern tip of Clapham Common and within the Old Town. The location benefits from a wide range of amenities including: Clapham Picture House cinema, Clapham Library, Clapham Leisure Centre.

This is salesman talk. The Picture House is in Venn Street, the Library in the High Street, and the Leisure Centre in Clapham Manor Street, all a kilometre away. The description of the actual building reads –

A refurbished single storey building fitted out to shell and core condition with WC facilities and with potential for outside seating area (subject to planning).

With WC facilities! Thou jestest! It was a WC!

24 JOHN DIXON

Later an artist's impression shows the building as it might be. All windows were removed, two narrow doors in the former Gents, and the front and side walls of the Ladies totally removed. There is an entrance ramp.

Tempting? Still no takers. The building was boarded up, in the jokey advert style, imitation ivy and creeper, painted on. Was there a sunflower made into a smiling face? Perhaps. The hoardings were very high. Too high to scale. Too high to see over. Impossible to find a peep-hole.

Then the hoardings were eventually removed to reveal a pile of rubble, quickly cleared and paved over. A circle of benches was added, a few individual seats, plus more mature shrubs and more spindly trees.

The restaurant – once the betting shop – acquired an extra floor, quite out of keeping with the lower floors and adjacent buildings. One or other of the various owners of the restaurant must surely at some stage have made representations to the Council that a public toilet near a restaurant was just not the thing. Did a bit of free wining and dining – who knows? – have clinched a gentleman's agreement. The restaurant is obviously doing well (a bottle of St Emilion, 1995, costs £1,400) and in the Post-Covid world the outside tables spill out almost as far as the site of the former toilet. Has the fashionable restaurant now become the place where the big knobs hang out?

The spindly trees have trunks too small to afford privacy were you to piss up them – but pissed up they will undoubtedly be.

One of the immovable seats is almost above the old toilets. It's not as comfortable as a lavatory seat but passable enough to allow a half hour's reflection.

Nearby is a large isolated man-hole cover – the last vestige of the toilet.

The Biograph Boys
Jeffrey Doorn

Joey took a seat one in from the left aisle just as the film began. He had wanted to see *The Boys in the Band* since it first came out four or five years ago, and was glad when he heard it was playing here in the Biograph. As a bonus, it formed part of a double bill with another film he hadn't seen. The cinema, in Wilton Road, was very convenient, as it was not far from the shop where he worked, and near Victoria Station, where he caught his train home.

He was aware of the cinema's sleazy reputation as a cruising ground; and sure enough, he noticed a lot of seat-changing going on. Occasionally he heard the banging of a door across the auditorium, presumably the toilet, where, by all accounts, more action took place. While in principle he had nothing against a bit of hanky-panky, he was there to see the film and its depiction of gay life. One or two men in the row in front turned to peer at him; but he ignored them and concentrated on the screen.

So absorbed did he become in the story and characters, he was not at first aware that someone had taken the aisle seat next to him. When he registered the presence he allowed himself a glance and noted it was a young man, a bit shorter than himself, and, from what he could judge in the dim light, nice-looking. It occurred to him that the cinema was not so dark as others; presumably this was the management's unsuccessful attempt to prevent naughty activity.

Joey turned his attention back to the screen, but couldn't help wondering whether the young man had come mainly for the film or for other purposes. Out of the corner of his eye he noticed the lad turn his head to look at him; Joey turned and met his eyes. They smiled then faced the screen again. Moments later their fingers touched and soon they were holding hands. Joey felt a stirring, but somehow didn't want to spoil things by having fumbling sex there in the cinema. His companion seemed sweet and innocent, and Joey savoured the romance of the moment.

As he continued to watch the film, an alternative film began running in his head. In this scenario, the pair would sit like this to the end of the film, briefly discuss it and perhaps even stay for the second feature. Joey would then invite his new friend for coffee; things would go on from there, making love, further dates, building to a romantic affair, though begun in so unromantic a venue. They would laugh about it in years to come.

All these lovely thoughts were broken when Joey realised someone had moved to sit on his right. A quick glance revealed the intruder was a man with dark curly hair. Joey fixed his attention on the screen, hoping the newcomer would keep his hands to himself. His hopes were in vain, as a paw began feeling its way up his right leg. How could he extract himself from this situation without causing a disturbance, upsetting his lover-to-be and getting all three of them thrown out? Should he whisper 'no thanks' or 'I'd rather not, if you don't mind'? What was the etiquette? While trying to think of a strategy, his trousers were being unzipped and the alien hand reaching in. He tried to brush it away, but Curly grasped Joey's right hand and moved it to his own erection before returning to extract and work on Joey's.

Still holding hands with the lad on his left, and feeling there was no escape from the hand on his right, Joey closed his eyes, thinking if he could come quickly, Curly would go away. Thoughts of the young man whose hand he gripped tighter, combined with his nervousness caused him to ejaculate. Curly withdrew his semen-soaked hand, covered himself up and moved to another seat. The lad turned his head, immediately taking in what had happened. His face registered disgust; he stood up and left the cinema. Joey had an impulse to follow, apologise, try to make it up; but he was too ashamed and embarrassed. He wiped himself with a handkerchief and zipped up. The film ended.

(The Electric Theatre opened 1909 at 47-48 Wilton Road SW1. Reconstructed 1927, it reopened as the Biograph Cinema with 630 seats. Popular with gay men from the 1960s, it was closed and demolished 1983.)

Two Poems
Jill Gardiner

Night Off

The bell. I watch her down the stairs.
Her slicked back hair, the leather tie.

One look she gives me. What I am
she knows. I stare. I smoke. I wait.

Some guy hollering outside the door:
'All you girls need is one good fuck!'

In here we're free. 'Are you a member?'
When women dare, a locked door opens.

She's there. I pull a Gitane from the pack.
Her flame flickers. 'Babe, wanna dance?'

'If this was really the only world,'
I whisper at her cheek. 'It is, it is.'

Mounting the staircase, I am Dietrich
all satin, and here is Garbo at my side.

Dining Out

In a vintage photo-book a friend has given me,
a crowd of 'Fifties women we'd love to meet:
shoulder to shoulder, in ties and trilbies, lipstick,
they're beaming: 'Cheese!' Their fags are glowing.
There's a forest of bottles, on a white-cloth table,
and a goblet of chocolates is circulating.

Women like us have always found a way.
Some eyes just met. Arm in arm they promenaded.
They'd grin at the attendant in the petrol station,
wiping her hands on her clean brown overalls;
or admire the pinkie ring on the usherette's finger.
The name of 'that club' was whispered, ear to ear.

And here we are tonight, in our fancy best:
a beret, a fedora, two dresses, linen trousers,
a waistcoat, you in stripes my silk scarf flowing,
at the Hotel du Vin, where the waiter's attentive
and doesn't bat an eyelid when the girls start chanting,
demanding that we dance the Gateways Grind for them.

We may have it all now from Gaydar to marriage:
You pick up the iPad and film without asking,
the shirts are open-necked, the couples dancing,
but nothing beats a party in a private room,
where, family of choice, we can let our hair down,
and know we're loved, whatever. Just like then.

Originally published in *With Some Wild Woman:
Poems 1989–2019* (Tollington Press)

On Railton Road, a Queer Walking Tour
Ian Townson

I lived in Brixton from 1974 to approximately 1984 in a squatted gay community on Railton and Mayall Roads and I conduct the Queer Walking Tour of Brixton to keep alive memories of long-lost buildings, people and events. For most of the tour I evoke the ghostly presence of buildings that either have been demolished or used for a different purpose. Mostly set in the 70s though shading into 1981, a year in which Railton Road was the epicentre of the Brixton uprising, I travel through time and space to build up a picture of that long-lost era of radical politics. I should be clear that the tour is not exclusively about LGBT+ groups and individuals. I also include the considerable number of straight radical/revolutionary organizations in and around Railton Road.

Beginning at Herne Hill station at the southern end of Railton Road, after outlining explosive political events of the 70s compared to the more subdued present, our first port of call is the Commercial public house opposite the station. This is one of several pubs we were thrown out of for coming out loud and proud as gay. We did this either by holding hands, a peck on the cheek, wearing drag or sporting a chest full of gay badges. The point being three-fold; it was good for individuals to come out of the shadows into the light, it was good for those less able or willing to come out to see others fighting our corner, it was two fingers up at the authorities at a time when we were still illegal. We could be arrested for gross indecency, importuning for an immoral purpose or conspiracy to corrupt public morals, among other laws that the police could dredge up. Apart from mumbling and grumbling about our fate we didn't do anything further about our ejection, unlike the other pubs we were thrown out of which we will come to later. A favourite slogan around at the time was: 'Better Blatant than latent.'

Moving along Railton Road we come to a mural painted on the gable end of the 198 Contemporary Arts and Learning Centre. The mural depicts many individuals, organisations and political demands based in and around Railton Road from the early seventies to the late 1990s which are all mentioned later on the walk.

Further along we come to one of three women's centres on Railton Road at number 207, now converted into private dwellings. Squatted by women anarcho-feminists, the building housed a Claimants' Union for those on welfare benefits and the local squatters' group. A Men's Group (Against Sexism) also met there. The women who ran the locally based centre were more concerned about the immediacy of housing people, providing a creche and a working bath for unplumbed squatters, not least to mention fighting evictions and abuses by the welfare benefits system.

The Hamilton Supermarket at number 128 was once the Hamilton Arms, another public house we were thrown out of. David Callow's harmless peck on the cheek meant we were asked to leave. This time we went beyond grumbling and staged a 'sit in' backed up by squatters and a couple of left Labour councillors who joined the occupation. The police were called and all were dragged out of the pub onto the pavement including the Labour councillors. We weren't reinstated. The Race Today Collective also used the pub as their drinking establishment.

St. Jude's Parochial Hall adjoining the Primary School at number 213 is still there in one piece and the place where Brixton Faeries Theatre Group performed a Christmas cabaret/pantomime for local pensioners and girl guides. An eclectic mix of extracts from Bloolips' interpretation of Oscar Wilde's *Salomé* and a gay interpretation of *Sleeping Beauty* with girl guides at the end of the performance holding up signs saying 'Increase Pensions Now!' How about that for community involvement. Probably performed around 1978/79.

We move along to the Brixton Advice Centre at

number 167 which is still operational though in a much reduced capacity because of cuts in funding and legal aid. A severe blow given that the centre was established by Labour member Maureen Boyle in the early 70s specifically for the needs of the most disadvantaged people dealing with debt, immigration, community care, asylum, mental health, housing and employment among others. The centre has charitable status but is struggling.

The Race Today Collective squat was just around the corner from Brixton Advice Centre at 74 Shakespeare Road. Breaking through a wall in 1980 a second squat was established at 165 Railton Road. Leila Hassan, Darcus Howe, Farrukh Dhondy, Olive Morris, Linton Kwesi Johnson, all members of the British section of the revolutionary Black Panther Party, edited the *Race Today* magazine and campaigned against racial discrimination and racist police violence and deaths in police custody. Notable are their involvement in the Mangrove nine, The Black People's Day of Action, the Notting Hill Carnival and the Brixton Uprising. C. L. R. James, the revolutionary socialist thinker and activist, spent his last days living and being cared for by the collective. His spouse, Selma James, founded the English Collective of Prostitutes and the Wages for Housework campaign. A blue plaque in memory of C. L. R. James was unveiled at 165 Railton Road in 2004. One to Darcus Howe was put in place by Nubian Jak Community Trust in 2022. No longer a hive of revolutionary activity 165–167 is up for sale as office space for the princely sum of £1,400,000, and 74 Shakespeare Road is a terraced house valued at £879,000, the most expensive in the area.

Our next port of call is the gay community squats on Railton and Mayall Roads consisting of about nine or ten houses. They were redeveloped as single person units when the squatters formed a gay section of the Brixton Housing Co-operative. The households run parallel with each other with a shared garden in between. We visit the garden as part of the Queer Walking Tour of Brixton.

There is a plaque at number 151 Railton Road, originally part of the gay squats, celebrating the achievements of Rotimi Fani-Kayode, a multi-talented black gay photographer. He was influenced by Robert Mapplethorpe's earlier work but also pushed the bounds of his own art, exploring sexuality, racism, colonialism and the tensions and conflicts between his homosexuality and his Yoruba upbringing through a series of images in both colour and black and white. He fused images of Africanness with Queerness with subtlety, beauty, irony and social and political comment.

Number 103 Railton Road is now private flats. Back in the 1970s, Pearl, a robust black bisexual woman originally from Jamaica, ran an illicit shebeen specifically for black gay men. This was at a time when racist white owners of drinking establishments barred black people and black gay men were not welcome in their own 'community'. White gay friends were also welcome and people from the Brixton gay community socialized there.

Private dwellings now stand at number 82 Railton Road which used to be the George public house. The landlord was notorious for banning black people and was prosecuted under the Race Relations Act. Brixton gays were thrown out and banned permanently and Mrs Old, the landlady, was featured in Brixton Faeries play *Mr Punch's Nuclear Family*. The pub was destroyed during the Brixton Uprising of 1981. We were not sorry to see it disappear.

We squatted the South London Gay Community

Centre at 78 Railton Road in March 1974. The centre lasted for two hectic but very productive years. The building was demolished as was the Women's Place at number 80 which, among other things, was the HQ of the National Abortion Campaign. A decision has now been made to memorialize the centre with a rainbow plaque at the site. There were originally several gay squats in St George's Residences immediately behind the gay centre.

At 65 Railton Road Olive Morris, a member of the Black Panthers and prominent in the local squatters' movement, squatted the first ever Black Women's Centre with Liz Obi; it is now private flats.

The Windsor Castle public house on Leeson Road, just off Railton Road, was also burned to the ground during the 1981 Brixton Uprising. This was the fourth pub that Brixton gays had been thrown out of for coming out as gay and as with the others we were not sorry to see it disappear.

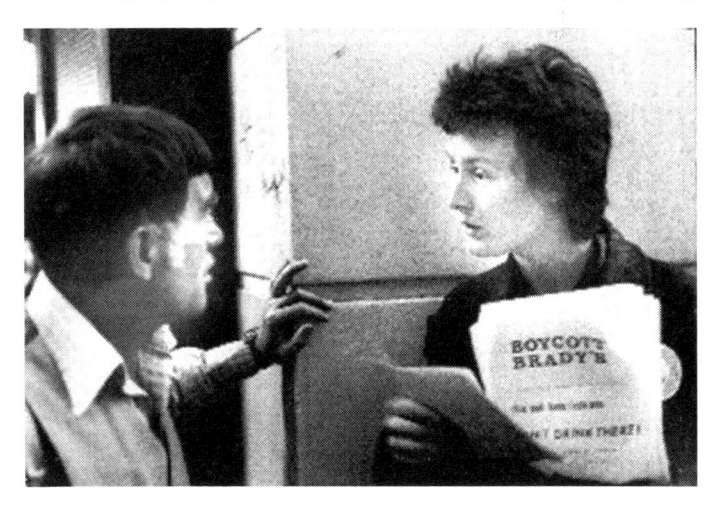

Leaving Railton Road we now turn into Coldharbour Lane where the brand new Brixton House theatre space has been built on previously derelict land. Replacing the Oval House Theatre which was based at the Kennington Oval, Brixton House carries on the tradition of producing radical Black, LGBT+ and Women's theatre. Next door is the hugely impressive 'Nuclear Dawn' mural depicting the cold war threat of nuclear annihilation including Margaret Thatcher's complicity in allowing the siting of cruise nuclear missiles at Greenham Common.

The Railway Tavern on Atlantic Road, better known as Brady's, was picketed by Brixton gays and others to protest against the barring of lesbians. The pub was redeveloped and is now a branch of Mexican-style restaurants.

The London Queer Social Centre was squatted in the 2010s in the Joy abandoned clothing store on Coldharbour Lane which has now been redeveloped as a branch of Premier Inn hotels. During the squat's precarious and short existence the intrepid class war warriors held workshops, campaign meetings, parties, film shows, built accommodation, cooked delicious food and defiantly opposed the police.

I mention the Prince of Wales just further up from the LQSC almost at the juncture of Coldharbour Lane and Brixton Road. Once a gay bar it is now straight and was split in two, with one half now housing a Kentucky Fried Chicken branch.

Our final destination for part one of the tour is Windrush Square in the centre of Brixton where I discuss the following in the square itself:

1. The Ritzy cinema where we held a picket for Jamie Dunbar from the Brixton gay community who was sacked in 1981 for wearing gay badges and demanding fair working conditions among other things.

2. The Tate Library which held a Brixton gay commu-

nity exhibition in the mid-1970s.

3. The Gents toilets (closed for many years) as the site of cottaging with graffiti and contact details on the walls for sex.

Across the road from Windrush Square is Lambeth Town Hall where we held many successful discos and dances as fundraisers for the South London Gay Liberation Front and various campaigns throughout the 1970s and early 1980s.

Finally in 1973 we were forced to leave the crypt of St Matthew's church, wedged between Effra Road and Brixton Hill, by hostile, misguided youths and users of the community centre who didn't want us there. The crypt has been variously used as a night club and a restaurant.

Please note: The history of the Brixton gay community and the South London Gay Liberation Front is much more comprehensively covered in the new website:
www.revoltinggays.com

Obituary: Chariots, Shoreditch
Zekria Ibrahimi

So many gay venues in London are being wiped out by the savage greed of the capital's ruthless and relentless developers.

The account books of cruel property magnates are incapable of factoring in such terms as 'love', 'community', and 'pride'.

On the way to 'The Glory', the brave, civilized queer beacon daring to illuminate bland and bleak Haggerston, I saw with shock from the number 149 bus that one more gay haven full of light and hope had been closed down.

Chariots, in Shoreditch.

The obviously cute place with painted pillars next to Majestic Wines.

It has been extinguished. The love it had protected is now dispelled like scented vapour disappearing into cold, hard frost.

Instead of East End gay men cruising for affection and togetherness in this sauna always seeming safe and welcoming, there are now gritty builders, with yellow donkey jackets and grey helmets, dismantling casually what had been a queer hyper-paradise.

Let us mourn Chariots – and let us campaign, I ask you all, for the noble, and still threatened, gay institutions that impersonal corporations want to exterminate in the hateful name of money!

The Sauna, as sweet as its sweat!
The place where love, like fiercest summer,
Is chanced upon, found, seen and met ...
I, at first, think about each plumber,

Each brick-layer, who formed this place,
From mundane plans, precise and cold.
And did the architect's grey face,
Amidst the designs in his hold,

Not show love, warm, giving and kind,
Not glow like fire, to indicate
Beauty's mansion he had in mind,
His to conceive, his to create?

Chariots. Shoreditch. I go there.
The Central Line. Liverpool Street.
The ticket office takes my fare.
What am I looking for? Just meat?

Just fried portions of vapid cock,
Spread out as in a butcher's shop?
The time is evening. Eight o'clock.
Is love like sirloin or pork chop,

Is love carcasses to be shown
To the butcher wielding a blade,
Is love blood and muscle alone,
Sold by the pound, cut up, displayed?

I ponder, near Majestic Wines.
I walk on, a matter of yards,
Beneath each tall street lamp that shines.
I think of what's now on the cards –

Sex as king – and love seems the ace.
The queer, the joker in the pack,
Fears isolation, cold disgrace,
The thug's sneer and taunt and attack,

The divorce from togetherness,
The contempt, and then yet more violence;
He trembles, hammered by distress,
Weeping alone, in shame and silence.

It is like being crucified,
When you're a gay, and isolated.
Queer-bashers don't allow you pride –
You're frightened, bullied, decimated-

So Chariots seems Resurrection,
It's coals, laughter, community,
It is love's transfigured perfection –
Love is wherever queers may be.

From West London, to the East End.
And Chariots, a mini-palace,
Lover with lover, friend with friend,
Reminds me of a Pompeii phallus –

You know, perhaps, from photographs,
In books about that dear doomed town,
Dicks inscribed into stone – for laughs –
Or to show the way – left, right, down –

To all the grubby tenderness
Of the local brothel. I meet
A pile of soiled towels in a mess
In a basket – after, I greet,

Next to them, lounging at Reception,
An attendant. 'That'll be twelve pounds,'
He says ... Love does not brook deception –
Mere lies are what love mocks and hounds –

Love abhors cheating, in the end –
But love accepts it has a price ...
Twelve pounds, that's cheap. Let me intend-
Nearness, affection, soothing, nice.

Twelve pounds – what is that, as a sum?
Money is nothing, love is all.
This attendant's rarely glum –
He's love too, he's love's Rise and Fall,

He's love, saga and paradox,
Its disappointment, and its pleasure,
Its caresses, and its hard knocks,
He's love, he's all its off-hand treasure.

He smiles back, and turns away
To each noisy washing machine;
Love is love, whatever you pay-
Love is love, if not always 'clean'.

I undress, in the locker room;
Nudity is democracy.
Now only cocks and arses loom.
Our joy, peril? – is being free.

It's all anonymous and fun-
It isn't conformist, it's risk.
It's twelve pounds, and for everyone.
And the business it does is brisk.

Some may be old, some may be plump,
Some butch, some camp, some average only,
Some with a birthmark on the rump,
And many, many, must be lonely.

What drives us queers, to such a site?
Just the hope to suck someone's dick?
To witness lust's brash flames alight?
To scan an arse, for one more trick?

The steam-room is where we may grope,
Half-glimpsing, half-blind, next to love.
Closeness, lush yet not tame, *is* hope;
The heat gathers, below, above.

I wank someone; he wanks me back;
The spunk exits, all sour white –
Love is sly, like a gambler's knack,
Winning the danger of delight.

I lounge in a cabin; I wait,
For a stray fuck to wander in.
Condemn us, with the tools of hate –
Those sham words such as 'vice' and 'sin'!

Are we being stewed in our Hell?
But love *ought* to be crude and raw,
An unkempt beast with its own smell,
Bound to bite back at any law.

Love is not fancy etiquette,
Like some scrubbed cherub in the sky.
It should be wild, then wilder yet –
Always seeking rules to defy. ...

Some ignore me, and some are curt;
I am no twink who finds love easy;
To lack a shag means so much hurt –
Or, at least, makes me odd and queasy.

I fill a guy's arse, for a while,
Then he walks off, laughs by the pool –
Stray sex deserves a wink and smile.
Morning comes, and love has to cool –

The red coals dwindle and diminish;
This session ceases, like all joys.
Even love is fated to finish –
I re-enter Bishopsgate's noise,

Near Liverpool Street, and descend
Into the tube, and return 'home' –
Or is home *love*, which, in the end,
Is Chariots? There, we can roam,

Like molecules of H_2O,
Rampant at one hundred degrees,
Cruising, colliding, with a flow
That looks like energy at ease ...

I'm older, in my run down flat,
On an armchair, tattered and worn ...
Years dribble on ... Where I once sat,
In Chariots, looking reborn,

Baptized by sulphur in the steam,
Is now lost rubble, scourged by spite.
Developers tore down the dream –
Older, I feel shock at the sight ...

The mock-Roman façade is gone,
Replaced by scaffolding instead.
Workmen in jackets hurry on,
Like shadows of relentless dread,

Not gay men, towels around their waist,
Joking, lounging, saying: 'Let's fuck.'
Please, mock greed, with such apt distaste –
Mammon, which kills love, is sick muck.

Builders had once fashioned this spot
As love's meadow, in a bleak town –
Builders, paid not to care a lot,
Now smash our rose-crammed Eden down.

'Once' and 'now' are such different terms,
'Once' and 'now' can be like a curse,
And something in my soul soon squirms,
As at the approach of a hearse.

The most brutal winter usurps
The former brave Empire of Love –
No bird, nestling in passion, chirps –
No Sun, kissing hearts, reigns above.

Why is love made to fade, to die,
Love, precious like a gentle tear?
And something in me needs to cry.
The ghost of love is weeping here.

The Viking, Birmingham
Leigh V. Twersky

The Viking, Birmingham, alas no more.

Summer 1974, the Viking was my first taste of a gay pub after having a crush on Peter T., whose reaction to falling for me was taking an overdose and running back home to Sheffield.

Tragic ... I ended up with Tony Mac.

At 75 Smallbrook Queensway in the centre of Birmingham, The Viking was a small, modern, cube-shaped cellar-bar accessed via a staircase and a welcome – and welcoming – gay haven compared to the slightly seedier Vic round the corner. At that time there was a weird Sunday closing time of 9 p.m. because of the Quakers, who had some say in such matters.

Oh, the regulars – I wonder what became of Graham, Trevor, Barry and all the others.

One fine evening, December 1974, I was sitting with friends at a table facing the stairs. I had a drink, but no home as my flat had just burnt down.

The night before I'd spent at my affair Adrian's place – we didn't say partner in those days – so I'd let Tom, a friend with various issues, stay at mine. I remember walking home in the morning, presciently wondering what damage Tom might have caused, so I wasn't too surprised to see smoke billowing out of the window and a few moments later Tom milling about dazed in the street. Victoria Road, Harborne, by the way. He'd made himself an omelette and left the electric hob-thing on. All night. The landlady demanded me and my flatmate repaint the flat but backed down when we pointed out the wiring was faulty.

'Well, terminate the residency,' she said.

Tom was okay. No one died.

So, there I was, sat in the Viking, nursing my drink, making it last, as you do, when I hear this almighty bang. Next thing I know I'm covered from head to toe in glass chips.

Then I see the faces of the men on the stairs, who'd hurled their pint glasses at us, and hit the wall inches above our heads. And the hatred in their stare before they legged it.

Did they aim to miss to merely frighten us…or were they just lousy shots?

Following the briefest of shocked silences, (although I think someone did mutter 'Fuck me'), the entire pub chased after them, but by the time we'd got upstairs, they'd already disappeared far into the night.

Fortunately, their dimpled pint mugs were thick glass, which smashes into rounded chips — relatively harmless — and not the type that shatters into lethal shards.

From that moment on, things could only get better. I moved in with Barry (not an affair) in Longbridge. And I'd never before had an address with a road number over a thousand, like in America.

Evenings at the Viking usually continued at the Nightingale, a club then in Camp Hill but later in Witton Lane, Aston, reached on the 39 bus. We bopped our troubles away to the disco faves of the 70s till the early hours: 'Don't Leave Me This Way', 'Young Hearts Run Free', 'TSOP', 'I Feel Love', 'Rock Your Baby', 'Shame Shame Shame', 'Feel The Need In Me' and so many others. One-night stands largely forgotten. Some good enough to repeat. I believe the club might still exist. Not at that venue, but somewhere in the second city.

The Viking is now a café bar, the Sunflower, but haunted I'm sure by the spirit of its former incarnation.

***

A gents' toilet condom machine, SW5

The Bolton's, Earl's Court. The venue is still going under the name of The Boltons & Proeflokaal Rembrandt, specializing in Dutch and Belgian beers, alas no longer gay and temporarily closed at the time of writing because of Covid-19. It has survived various reincarnations as both a Victorian dining hall and an O'Neill's Irish-themed pub. In the 1970s it complemented the nearby Coleherne, but by the 1980s had acquired a somewhat seedy reputation.

How I chuckled one evening in the late 1970s at graffiti on the condom machine:

WASTED HERE, I FEAR!

Little did we know then how poignant those words would be just a few years later …

The Last Gold Star Lesbian
V. G. Lee

There was this woman I really liked. She's been dead five years now and I've never allowed myself to grieve. It didn't seem appropriate – you see she didn't belong to me although I don't think she ever truly belonged to anyone and that would include her long-term partner. We met fleetingly in London during the 1990s but I didn't get to know her in any depth at that time. I was recovering from an affair that had gone very wrong and my confidence was at rock bottom.

Some years later I read an article in a magazine about the influx of lesbians into Hastings, Hebden Bridge and Hackney. I'd already spent two decades living in and around Hackney, West Yorkshire was too far north for my thin London skin and so I moved to the south coast: a house on a hill with a distant view of the sea if I stood on the bench at the foot of my garden! I didn't discover lesbians in the quantity the magazine promised but I did begin to tentatively establish a fresh life for myself. By then I was in my fifties and still single. As a pessimistic soul I was much aware that the serious years were approaching and I'd have to face them alone. As time passed, this affected my spirits like a chill draught between the shoulder blades. And then one day, as I waited at the 28 bus stop for a ride up the West Hill to visit a friend, a vintage Jaguar saloon car pulled up – on the zebra crossing – outside Marks and Spencer's. I recognised the long-term partner – she still wore the deep red lipstick that made her lips look swollen. My gaze moved to the driver's window. All I could see were strong tanned hands, a glimpse of white shirt cuff. The bus came. By the time I'd settled in my window seat, the Jag had gone.

That one sighting down in Hastings town centre put me on red alert. If the woman and her partner had moved to the town, it would soon be mentioned on the local lesbian grapevine. Sure enough information began to pour in: *a fantastic, rich, gorgeous, two-car owning couple have moved into a detached house with extensive gardens and massive gazebo sited in the salubrious Clive Vale area.* I did not declare a vested interest. I smiled when given this information, raised one eyebrow – quizzically – and kept listening.

I was never anything much in the looks department although I've often been told I have nice eyes, as if that's adequate compensation for all the rest that's lacking. But if I do have a 'unique selling point' it would be that I can make people laugh. I used to despair of only having this one talent on offer but since many of my peers often greet me with a list of aches and pains and complaints about the weather, I'm able to lighten the encounter with a good joke, cheer 'em up, find something amusing to cover almost any situation. I've been referred to as 'a tonic'! Nowadays I'll take 'nice eyes' and being a 'tonic' as worthwhile compliments!

By the time she settled in Hastings, my Gold Star lesbian was well past her glorious best, but still a zillion times more attractive than anyone I've ever known. Her face was expressive: a lived-in face, not beautiful, not handsome. There was something about her; call it charisma, put it down to self-confidence which she possessed in buckets – but what really stood out was her love for women! When she turned her attention on you or me – oh god – it was as if I'd endured fifty years as a scrunched up flower before finally uncurling my petals to the warmth of the sun!

Next to Hastings Library was a café. Once a month between thirty and fifty women met up for a meal and afterwards the chairs and tables would be pushed aside and we'd dance to all the old favourites: Abba, Tina Turner, Gloria Gaynor, Dusty Springfield. We were mostly middle to late middle-age, in most cases opting for comfort dressing rather than glamour, bringing along our cardigans or fleeces just in case the night turned chilly. Rumour had it that this particular evening, the new arrivals on Hastings gay scene would be attending. I'd made a special effort: pink slim-line shirt with pink satin tie, cream baggy trousers with belted waist: the outfit emulating the sort of vintage vibe of Diane Keaton in the film, *Annie Hall* released three decades earlier.

There was a long queue at the counter for the dinner: a set meal of roast chicken with all the trimmings. I don't recall a vegetarian option. This may well have been before vegetarian options became optional! In the queue were the usual handful of moaning minnies who preferred lamb or sausages or battered cod. I decided to wait till the line shortened rather than look too eager about the eating side of the evening. Time passed, but there was no sign of the woman and her partner. Surreptitiously, I kept an eye on the front door. Everyone else had arrived. There were just the two spare place settings on my table. At any moment Marilyn or Elsie – perfectly nice women – would suggest they close up the space. 'Wouldn't want you sitting on your own,' one or the other would insist.

The door swung open and in they came. The live-in-lover swathed in a lacy shawl immediately began making apologies to the organiser, citing the diversion of traffic on Queen's Road for their lateness. Of course it was fine for them to be late. They were the stars of the evening. I had to admit that both women looked wonderful: polished, burnished – as if they'd stepped off a luxury cruise liner!

Up till then, it hadn't occurred to me that I was slumping in my chair but now I straightened up, shoulders back, face flatteringly tilted towards the overhead light.

Elsie said, 'Aren't you eating? I can vouch for the chicken. It's delicious.'

Had I replied, I might have snapped, 'I'm here for something more exciting than the fucking chicken.' Instead I picked up my wine glass and got to my feet, heading for the wall at the back of the room. For once in my life I knew what I was doing. That one wall was painted blue. I saw myself as the unfurling flower of my imagination: pink and cream against a blue sky waiting to be plucked.

The partner peeled away to join the food queue. My Gold Star lesbian was arranging her coat over the back of her chair. Job done to her satisfaction, she looked around the room, passed me over but then her gaze returned. My mouth refused to form a smile. Actually I was near to tears. I felt such relief, as if a space between my breasts had opened up to allow my heart to show itself. As the queue parted letting her saunter towards me, I gulped a mouthful of wine, eyes lowered so she wouldn't see the hunger in them.

'Hello you. Long time no see,' she said. She planted the palm of her hand against the wall next to my head, her tanned wrist with gold gate-leg bracelet, almost brushing the side of my face: 'What a fucking shit hole this is!'

We both laughed. The room fell silent. Women turned to stare at us.

'Let's sit down.' Her voice was so gentle.

Sometimes after one too many glasses of wine, I muse on the possibility that I could have prised her away from the partner, but sober, experience tells me that when I'm really keen on someone, involuntarily I take a step backwards. The stronger my emotion, the more I fear failure. I listen to my head telling me: No way. Shut out the heart before it can get a word in edgeways. Each time we met afterwards – because we did meet, Hastings is a small town – I never followed the compulsion insisting that I blurt out, 'From the very first time I laid eyes on you at the Conway Hall, I've never been able to get you out of my mind.'

I kept my mouth shut believing that, 'Ta very much sweetheart, but you're punching far above your weight,' would be her most likely response.

I settled for a friendship of sorts that from time to time veered close to becoming something more. I was too timid but I also recognised that she'd maybe grown lazy, like an aging well-fed cat. She'd never had to try hard. Women literally dropped into her lap and why wouldn't they? She'd enjoyed an easy life, discounting a childhood which from all accounts was brutal. By the time our paths re-crossed, she was pretty much able to dine out on her accounts of past glory: stories of being a regular at The Gateways Club, how she'd known Dusty Springfield *very well* indeed, that when younger, Cilla Black actually sent her love letters! This might just have been alcohol talking – but if it was true, how amazing was that? Imagine if she'd hung on to Cilla's letters! I actually put the woman and some of her exploits into the novel I was writing at the time, turning her into a comic figure, making her unrecognisable. Fortunately she never read any of my books, very few people did. She had a passion for violent crime novels whereas a critic once described my writing as 'Barbara Pym on Aspirin'.

What more can I tell you? I have a pair of Urban Stone jeans she bought me ten years ago. They still fit snugly although the leg shape's a bit weird for modern styling. There was nothing romantic about the purchase and I wasn't the only woman she bought clothes for. She liked to shop and if you were with her – and she knew I didn't make much money – she'd insist you choose something. I don't think I'll ever get rid of those jeans. At least once a year, I fish them out to wear. I might even stipulate in my Will on being buried in them!

On that momentous evening at the café in Hastings, I was just one of many women she was attentive to. When she wasn't dancing or drinking – I didn't see her eat a thing – she smoothed her way around the room paying particular attention to those she was attracted to. To my knowledge she never did anything about the attraction. You could say she was all talk, no action but I believe she made a conscious decision not to act. Sometimes my gaze rested on the partner who in her way was equally sociable – but not flirtatious. I'd have liked to ask about their history, where and how they'd met. I didn't ask. Again, feeling the way I did, as if I'd sacrifice anyone and anything to have the woman I wanted, it seemed inappropriate.

I'm nearing the end of this brief memoir, returning to that first encounter in London. Only a matter of weeks earlier I'd emerged from the clandestine affair that destroyed my confidence. To cheer me up, a friend treated me to a ticket for a dance at the Conway Hall. The friend danced every dance while I remained at the table sipping wine and trying to look sophisticated rather than lonely. It felt as if everyone in the crowded room recognised me as a misfit, confused straight woman out on the dabble!

'Dance?'

I looked up and there she was offering me her hand: butch lesbian wearing a beautifully tailored dress suit with a scarlet cummerbund. I was clumsy getting to my feet. She placed her hand on my elbow to steady me.

I've no idea what song we danced to other than it was slow and required her to take me in her arms. I remember how the close proximity of our bodies disturbed me: my breasts against her chest, her lips touching my forehead. When the music stopped she led me back to my chair.

'Later?' she said.

I nodded.

But there was no later. The friend who'd brought me fell ill. I went outside to hail a taxi. When I returned, someone with red, luscious lips was tugging the woman onto the dance floor. 'It's a Rumba,' I heard her say. 'The dance of love.'

I took a step towards them.

My woman turned her head, absorbed the coat over my arm, handbag hanging limply at my side. She gave me this rakish smile, a sort of 'ah well' smile.

The friend tugged my arm. That was it. The moment lost.

Once she moved here, I'd see her on a regular basis over several weeks. Her company made me feel desirable and happy. She'd drop by for coffee – the running joke between us was my instant coffee – in her words – *tasted like shit!* Sometimes we'd spend an afternoon browsing in the Old Town, sometimes she'd drive us out to a garden centre. Foolishly I'd hope that someone would recognise me sitting in the Jag, in her partner's place. Nobody did. It would seem as if a mutually happy routine was established and then suddenly, silence. Some kind person would mention that she, her partner and their close friends had gone abroad, or she was seeing other women she shared similar tenuous relationships with. She never became a reliable fixture. I've thought since, how rare truly gorgeous women are: nowhere near enough of these fine creatures to go round, to enhance the lives of us lesser mortals.

After her funeral we all met at the same small café near the library. It was up for sale by then, the furniture and décor looking a bit battered and bruised. As I went in, I could almost hear her exclaiming: *what a fucking shit-hole*, although it really wasn't. The food had always been good, staff welcoming. It suited the town whereas the town never really suited the woman. Like the books in the library next door, she'd been on loan. London was her *milieu*, was where she should have lived and died.

On the wall behind the refreshment table a collage was pinned, pictures taken from the seven decades of her life. One in particular stood out. Everyone commented on it because it caught the essence of her, the laughing-at-herself bravura of the woman. She was in her mid-twenties, posing in front of a gleaming Harley Davidson motor bike. Black jeans, black leather jacket, white t-shirt and hair looking sexually rumpled – if you know what I mean. Iconic I thought – woman and bike – iconic.

That café's gone now. A kitchen shop has taken its place. If women still meet up monthly for dinner and disco, I'm unaware of it. These days I rarely go out in the evening. Why would I? There'd be no butch lesbian striking an insolent pose, smile lines and wrinkles between her eyes from squinting into the sun, no butch lesbian waiting for that femme fatale, the perfect match which I like to think, should have been, could have been me.

Idiot! Slaps forehead. Lays down pen. Reaches for tissues.

One-way Transaction
Adrian Risdon

(The former loo at Old Steine, Brighton is now Gossip in the Steine Café. I was accosted by the poem's speaker as I emerged from the underground cottage. He was lugging an enormous camper bag full of bottled booze.)

You gay? I'm bi. Go back into the gents.
Don't muck about, you're wasting time. Look here:
the fuzz can book us just for loitering.
So come on down. No – let the bag alone.
Incapable I'm not; and if I choose
I'll get through all these Guinnesses tonight.
Check the place out. I'll feather-bed the booze …
Here! By the stalls! Don't go all shy on me:
bollocksing's what you came for, Let's play fair:
it has to be the season; otherwise

what your sort does in public here, you'll do
snug in the bog at home. Queer-bashers, fuzz –
   all one to you! So long as your blood thrills
   to play the victim, you don't care who kills.

This cubicle will suit. No – stay where you are.
Assistance not required: I'm as young as you.
'Engaged'...but no one's in there. If a bloke
so much as pokes his prick in, he'll get done.
You too, if you'll not listen what you're told.
Study that fist: I don't get messed about.
Shuck down at once: I want to see the world...
Not bad. Half marks. Oh no, you'll not see mine:
tonight the wife's monopolizing me.
You've to supply the re-charge. Understand?
One-way transaction. And if we should meet –
in pubs perhaps, or down the Promenade –
   no signals, mate! no hints! Nothing thar smells
   of previous acquaintance, mush! Or else.

A one-night stand, this. Gottit? Good. Oh fuck
the crappy beer: I'm limp, I'm useless! Now
I'll have to tell her: 'Not tonight, I'm tired.'
or some such shit. You ever been with one?
You have? Not married are you? Thought not. Oh,
put it away. Doesn't do nothing for me ...
Boyfriend? You should push yourself. See here:
I married at 18. The law's the law:
why wait till 21 for what you want?
And she's not bad: give me a kid (he's mine):
cooks well, looks good. Curse of it is: she wants –

> *they* want laddie brought up Catholic...
>> I go to church. I sing the hymns... she's sure
>> my inclination's something Christ can cure.

Maybe He can; but one thing He – for all
His arms-outstretched-to-bless bit – shan't gainsay.
I told her straight: 'I'll trot along to Mass
if you'll put up with me and my drinking pals.'
Saint Mary's first; then off to The Green Man:
that's the arrangement. Curse of beer is, like
it makes you want to, sees to it you can't.
Know what I mean? Like ... useless! No you don't –
keep your frigging fingers to yourself!
If I weren't drunk, you'd pay for that. Okay –
so you're frustrated. Count yourself lucky, mate:
you're fancy-free; your time's your own; you aren't
> obliged to fit yourself in as and when ...
> not that you'd cut much ice among the men.

Going Back
David Downing

It's been a long time. I don't know how long exactly and if I've ever consciously counted it in years that's something I no longer do. I'm here now. I remind myself that the past is finished business.

So I'm unsettled by the recollections that have been intruding on the routines of my daily life. While I'm leaning on the gate watching the animals feed, there they will be, scenes from before. Silent yet animated. When I'm near done in the fields, or sitting alone by the fire in the evening, my mind will start playing its tricks and there they are again. Always catching me off-guard. Always from the same period, the same places. A time when things were different. They are not unhappy memories so I can't fully fathom why they have come back to haunt me now. Simple nostalgia perhaps, or degrees of curiosity; a reflex reaction to being so long-settled here. Who knows. In the end it's catharsis that seems to sit best with me. It suggests a process not wholly relished but somehow necessary. A form of healing.

I actually start to toy with the idea of going back. Not for ever, just a visit. Though I do nothing other than casually mull over the possibility before dismissing it.

Until.

An envelope arrives and I recognise-but-can't-place the handwriting. The note inside is short yet as unmistakeable as it is unexpected. It's from you. It gives me pause, as if the years of silence have suddenly been erased.

I'm pleased and reticent in equal measure, though your message serves to focus my thoughts of return and gives everything an inevitability. Perhaps you had been the catalyst all along. Now you have become the reason.

***

The rhythms of this rural life are less easy to walk away from than those of that old city one. Livestock creates dependencies and obligations, a workload that's unrelenting demands focus and attention, so I'm no longer free to just up and leave, not even for a weekend. But I'm humbled to discover that I've been here long enough now for favours to be considered unremarkable gifts and while that allows me to go it also makes me more reluctant to do so.

In the end, the physical journey turns out to be the easy part. Assorted engines doing the work for me, transporting me back. But it's the drivers of the internal journey that I'm still finding hard to reconcile. Then a small room in a chain hotel, tourist-generic, amongst the backstreets of the city that was once home, is a degree of alienation that tells me I no longer belong. And that isn't helping at all. I head out in search of something more familiar, towards streets I used to walk regularly, part of the network of my life. Back then. I see things differently now, of course. Overly observant, attuned to detail, noticing change where everything once felt so known and nuanced: grime where there used to be gleam; background noise that's relentless and intrusive rather than a vital part of the energy of things; the stink of refuse and unbreathable air that I don't recall; being so clumsily out of sync with the flow of people; shops selling things for which I no longer have use or need.

I start to wonder why I came.

With no particular destination in mind I slow my pace to a ramble and wander purposelessly in my old footsteps.

The not knowing, not being known, is partly what is unanchoring me, I decide. Where once these streets would have readily provided recognisable faces I now recognise no one, not even in passing. A shared glance of recognition, of I-knew-you-when, could be all it would take. The remnants of my family are still out there in the suburbs, somewhere, I presume, though I have long been refused permission to go back to where I'm not wanted. When some doors close they remain shut. But lots of people aren't around anymore, for any number of reasons, and I've lost touch with anyone who might have remained. Until you. I imagine I could make more sense of the changes if I could find something else familiar to tether myself to. I'm adrift and in need of connection.

I get the bus out of town, reassuringly still displaying the same route number that it used to, and that forms a fragile link between then and now. Old ways pass by the window. Many buildings remain unchanged, some gently refurbished and looking fresher, others standing entirely new in place of what I might once have recognised. The pavements are busy; lives are still being lived on the housing estates we pass; the short parades of local shops still serve customers old and new. This feels more like what I think I need. I get off at my once-regular stop but immediately feel like I'm trespassing. I follow the well-worn locals' shortcut, turn right onto the pavement I previously walked daily. On past houses some of whose owners' names I can still recall, before crossing the road to try to look less conspicuous as I glance over towards my old front door. Same but different. We lived there together for a while, you and I. You lived there still when I upped and left. Now within those walls new lives are playing themselves out. There's connection and separation, belonging and rejection, and these tensions leave me somewhat uncomfortable, embarrassed even, at finding myself here again and I hope no one has noticed. I don't linger. I walk on, niggled by foolishness and guilt, still willing for a sign that a part of this city recognises me, remembers, and is able to offer me a welcome back if not a welcome home. For some acknowledgement that I was here, then and now. But nothing is obliging. The sense of loss is compounding more keenly than it had ever done before I returned. I loiter by the river for a while then head back to wait for the bus into town.

Ambling again towards the hotel, not really taking things in, I'm lost in attempts to reassure myself that this wasn't what this trip was about anyway. Perhaps I'm even beginning to feel a little less uncomfortable with my new-found rootlessness. Freed by the anonymity. But then my focus turns again to you and I become aware that I just might have been preoccupying myself to avoid giving scrutiny to these thoughts, much as I have since you got in touch.

Regardless, I have little time now to dwell. I decide not to change, to go as I am. Relaxed. Casual. Take things as they come. I pick up my wallet and keys, pull on my jacket, and head off out again. This time to meet you.

***

There's the flutter of nerves in my stomach; the embers of an old excitement. But I'm starting to realise that it's not simply the anticipation of meeting you. Not entirely. It's also because of where rather than who. Somewhere that seemed so obvious when you suggested it that I hadn't really given it another thought, until now. Of course we would meet there. Where else?

The tube stop flashes into view through the windows and I move towards the door, like so many times before. Muscle memory has me turn left through the 'no entry' sign, up the steps a few people are walking down, and there's that old feeling of knowing the way, of confidence in belonging. I wind back into the mainstream, filing onto the escalators, and am carried up towards ticket barriers that didn't used to be there. Everything else is the same – I skip the detail. I am on autopilot towards the correct exit, up the final steps and out into daylight.

The sense of anticipation is overwhelming.

But I don't recall coming out into daylight before. It was always degrees of darkness. In fact I have no recollection of the actual weather back then at all. The traffic is mid-afternoon workday-busy whereas it always used to be later, quieter, when it was mostly solitary taxis passing through the night, rarely stopping. Maybe it's still like that after dark, though I already have my doubts. The block of 60s maisonettes with grubby windows is still standing; the red-doored fire station; the old redbrick pub, drunks staggering in and out, but it's too early for things to start getting nasty. I used to put my head down, pick up my pace and walk purposefully past, avoiding eye contact, alert to any sound or voice. Trying to be invisible. We'd all fast-learnt self-preservation back then. I sense myself automatically doing the same thing again and go with it. I am my old self and my new self all at once. It's thrilling. It always was.

The walk along the old street is longer than I recall. A line of buildings that I only recognise now I'm here; traffic lights I had forgotten. But that's not important.

As I turn the corner, it's there.

The black paint, the black boarded-up windows, the black set-back door with its retractable hatch through which you would be assessed while the thudding pulse of the music pounding at the walls and the noise of so many voices inside was already beckoning. Then the door opening onto this other world. The tangible sense of arrival. Like coming home. Family.

Except it isn't.

The paintwork's green, the windows clear and clean, only gentle music vaguely drifting out through the fixed-open door. The feeling of emptiness. It is so familiar yet so different.

I step inside and have to pause to take it all in, to absorb the unexpected.

I'm early. And so are you. Old habits.

It draws me back.

You are unmistakeable, regardless of time's passing, and I smile at the look of recognition in your eyes and the curve of your lips as you smile back. I beeline towards you and we hug, more familiarity than strangeness despite everything. I sense your body, same but different, and along with memories of closeness I register an awareness of distance. Old love and old hurt. I wonder if you sense it too. We reciprocate upbeat greetings and compliments but it's all a notch too loud, too enthusiastic, too fixed-grin back-of-the-mouth and no-chest. And then there's a lull, brief but inescapable, as if this is as far as we've rehearsed in our minds and we're at a momentary loss for direction. For years there's been nothing but time between us and we need to reorientate ourselves. I make gestures of getting drinks but you're already on your way to the bar.

Over our pints we work out that how-long-has-it-been is twenty-five years. Half my lifetime ago. We met when you were twice my age and now I'm as old as you were then. I like the arithmetic symmetry of it as we juggle around with the maths. I don't tell you that you are now older than both my parents when they died.

You have weathered life better than me, though you were always kinder to it than I was so I don't resent you for that. You're style and labels, right people, right places, flow and connection. Whereas I'm still army surplus, solitary, escape, but less shunt and stall than I once was. Perhaps I was always the country to your city but just didn't realise it. And now I understand that us meeting here is your concession to me, remembering my attachment to the place. You always knew me better than I knew myself.

You tell me of the chance encounters and coincidences that led you to being given my address. The word you use is: serendipity. And I feel comforted, validated even, knowing this unseen network still exists and remembers me enough to recognise my name after all this time. People who knew-me-when. Maybe this is the remembrance I was hoping for all along. And then I ask you why? And it's too intimate too soon. But you say you often wondered how I was, what I was doing. Wanting to know that I was safe. And happy. Those old emotions catch me in the throat. And we step away from them.

The obligatory summary of our lives over two-and-a-half decades has too few surprises and is disarmingly prosaic and I think we both feel that beneath the gloss we are missing some big show-stopping revelations. Inevitably perhaps, conversation turns to the do-you-remember common ground of when we met. But both our versions are sufficiently different that they could almost be about other people entirely. What we do agree on is where: right here. And we begin retro-fitting the club, peeling back layers of paper and paint, removing and replacing walls, reinstating the pool table even though we can't agree on whether it existed or not, boarding up the windows, turning the lights down and the music up, and filling it with men. We talk of the dancefloor downstairs, the VIP room upstairs to which you were invited but I never was. We recall the celebrities who would pass through, the names we all kept secret and do so still. The ghosts of the past must have heard us, sensed our presence, and it's as if the old club actually starts shapeshifting, emerging from the past. It's in me. I can see it, feel it, and I am transported back there. Every Friday night, that siren call as men emerged from dark streets, converging to get in before the door charge started at 10 p.m. Part of the ritual. We had both been coming here before we started coming here together, to drink, to dance, to chat to people we knew and people we didn't, and of course to find lovers who opened doors onto other worlds too. It was all part of the party.

We continue along the path these memories take us before we recognise where it is heading and although we both want to pull back it's already too late. With that something deep inside me kicks in, grabs at the opportunity before it is gone, and I don't realise the words are coming out of my mouth until I am hearing myself say them. In a tone that is solemn and sincere I am telling you that I am sorry. For the mistakes I made, for the secrets and the lies, for letting you down. And most of all for the betrayal. You deserved none of it. I apologise for being too proud and stubborn to accept your forgiveness and for compounding my guilt with spitefulness and leaving. For walking out and walking away. As the words come out unbidden, twenty-five years too late, I feel the release. You look at me and listen and wait. I see the understanding in your eyes and see that you know. You always knew. And you thank me for saying what I have said. You tell me you held no resentment, only confusion and regret, for a while. But things moved on and I should not have been so hard on myself for so long. And, of course, you are right, as you always were. Quietly strong and patient while I was none of those things. This place, coming back, has given me the chance to confront the ending I imposed on us. To make amends. To no longer leave regrets unanswered.

Still, I hadn't planned this at all.

I turn my look from you, casting my eyes around the club, and witness it fading back, fading away, the walls returning to where they were when I walked in, the pool table gone, the décor once again fresh and modern, the music quietening, the place almost empty. Through the windows I can see the world outside passing by in the late afternoon sun.

I take a deep breath. I don't know where all that came from and I'm not sure if I can pull us back. But you are reassuring and find the right words, gently lifting tone and subject until we both laugh and the tension eases.

We talk of happier times, of the good things we did together. We learn a little more about each other as we share these tales and the stories flesh out further as we draw in memories of other people. It's like old times.

When the place begins to fill with younger city folk fresh from work and lively with the weekend, we make our way out onto the street and towards a restaurant you know. This is new territory for us and we are no longer rooted safely in the past. It's fine, but as the food takes over the alcohol-given energy of earlier begins to falter. The unfamiliar begins to feel intrusive and after coffee we are out again into the night. You suggest another drink but I think I'm done. You offer to walk with me back to my hotel but, although I have been away a while, I recognise what that means and where it would lead and I make my excuses. You understand.

We say our goodbyes and our farewell hug is more relaxed, more real, than the one with which we greeted each other. We both realise assurances to stay in touch are unlikely to be kept, but the it-was-good-to-see-yous are heartfelt and genuine. You head away and I wait, knowing that looking back is an imperative and when you turn we raise our hands in farewell before you disappear between buildings. I repeat the walk of earlier, back towards the club, but this time on the other side of the road, the side that seems to have been rebuilt with smart glass office blocks and apartments. I observe from a distance now the pub drunks, the fire station, the people coming and going along the line of shops. Old and new side-by-side. And then I turn the corner and am once again looking over at the club. It's busy, the music louder, the lights shine bright through the windows and the melee of raised voices is brimming with energy and expectation. It spills out onto the street, something we could never do. Still, helped by the dark, for me the place is willing to regain once more something of its past self. If I let my mind wander I can see the windows darken, hear the beat of old music return, see the men – in ones and twos – emerging from the night and disappearing behind the black door. I smile to myself. Happy times. I feel good. Before the moment can fade, I say my silent thank yous to those walls. And turn and walk away.

I sleep well in the unfamiliar bed in the strange hotel and the city is bright and bustling when I awake. I could head out, make the most of the few hours I have left before I need to leave, but decide against it. Instead I turn my focus towards home. I call to check everything is OK and am reassured that I need not worry. I wasn't, I say. That was not why I called.

***

We keep in touch, for a while. You and I. But soon enough the silences grow longer.

A few years later you send me a photo, of the club, now nothing but rubble. Flats are going up on the site, you say. You're thinking about buying one. But it's not long after that I receive a message from someone I don't know. The message tells me that, well, that you are now no longer about either. I expect sadness but over time loss has become part of life and less remarkable for it. Everything moves on.

It's said we should never go back. Perhaps there's some truth in that but I'm not so sure, not if there's something to go back to, something to go back for. I know I have no regrets.

The rhythms of life, the dependencies and the obligations, continue to keep me busy here. I know people and they know me. I am content, happy even. The recollections no longer intrude upon my days, though every now and then I might invite them back in. Yet, while the memories remain, the past itself is finished business.

*'Going Back' reunites the two protagonists who first met in 'Waiting' (*The Best of Gazebo, *Paradise Press, 2012). The club is based on The London Apprentice, 333 Old Street, London which, from the 1970s, was a second home to many gay men and where the first meeting of the Terrence Higgins Trust took place. Though no longer open, the building still stands.*

Finding and Losing Lesbian Spaces in Brighton and Hove, and Beyond
Jill Gardiner

I moved to Brighton in 1983, in my early twenties, when I had no gay life at all. Having been in unrequited love with various straight women, I had no idea how to find someone who might be open to same-sex love. I had never knowingly spoken to a lesbian. I had not come across *Time Out* magazine, or anything about contemporary gay women except an article, called 'Lesbians: have you ever really tried to understand them?' in a copy of *19* magazine from 1973, with a sepia photo of a woman in a long white Biba, Victorian-style nightdress on the cover, which I found in a second-hand bookshop. While I read *Spare Rib* occasionally, I hadn't discovered lesbian clubs there either. If I plucked up the courage to flick furtively through *Gay Times* in a W. H. Smith's far from home, it was so clearly mainly for men that I rapidly gave up looking.

Enduring curiosity, however, had driven me to my first viewing of *The Killing of Sister George*, at the Watershed Arts Centre in Bristol, when I was a student; but I hadn't realised that the scenes shot in the Gateways depicted a real lesbian club that was still open, even though the director had helpfully inserted its address and phone number into the script. The main characters in the film felt old-fashioned, middle-aged and unlike me: neither Coral Browne, the most seductive, Susannah York, the youngest, nor Beryl Reid leaping into a taxi with nuns in it, inspired any erotic fantasies for me. Nor did I identify with the real contemporary lesbians, in a short documentary that followed, who seemed more boyish than I was. I had long hair, wore skirts to work, and red dungarees at weekends, painted my fingernails alternately red and blue and wore mascara, eyeliner, and red lipstick. When I looked round the audience at the end, I didn't dare speak to anyone, though I half-wished someone would speak to me. I felt curious, but not at home. So I vanished into the anonymity of the city, intrigued that lesbian clubs existed, but no nearer to finding one.

When I moved to the South coast, to take up a job, I found a room to rent in Hove, through the *Evening Argus*, and became very close to my landlady. We shared our life stories, selectively. We laughed a lot. We went to folk clubs and sang. We walked on the Downs. We hugged. We danced. We kissed. Then we confided in each other about more difficult bits of our lives. Unexpectedly, we ended up in a relationship. Through her I found a lesbian and gay social scene I just hadn't had any idea how to find before. I expected that there would be all these clubs teeming with women, but it wasn't like that at all. The sort of social life I found through her at first was mainly based in people's houses – parties, dinner parties – and, like her, consisted mainly of women at least 15 years older than me.

One of the Brighton friends she introduced me to was Pat, a smiling, red-cheeked Welshwoman, with shoulder-length blonde hair, and brightly coloured, sparkly clothes, who rarely stopped talking. Pat, with her French lover

Sabine, took a group of us on what she called an Earth Mysteries tour to reclaim for women the Long Man of Wilmington (a chalk fertility-figure engraved into the Downs), by doing a ritual and giving her pebble-nipples. I was so new to the lesbian scene that this transgressive introduction to the goddess religion just seemed like one more new experience among many. All the women there were quite hippyish, with longish hair: or in the case of Sabine, stylishly Parisian, with well-cut trouser suit, chunky rings, and felt trilby. When Pat wasn't writing her huge history of ancient matriarchal societies and religions, or earning a living as a lecturer, she loved swimming in the sea, and dancing at Caves, which she described to me as a lesbian club in a basement in Sillwood Street. I was dying to see it, so one evening, a group of us went.

The door was locked, and you had to knock to be let in. An entry phone was answered, and a peep hole opened. Pat's unmistakable voice and ruddy face got us in immediately. Inside, you descended a staircase into the unknown, with excitement mounting as the beat of the music grew louder. Then you were stopped in your tracks by being asked to sign in. All gay clubs were members' clubs, so, to keep their licence for drinking beyond pub hours, a member had to sign guests in. This first time, in all innocence, I gave my real name. Someone told me later that the police got to see the books, so I thought, 'Oh, what if my employers find out?' so next time I gave a different name. As I worked in education, I could have been sacked then if I had been known to be gay.

It was an underground world, in every sense, Caves, because it was done up to look like a cave, with stippled, textured white walls, shaped out of Artex, and flickering lighting to give you the feeling that you were underwater. There was a dance floor, but it was quite small, and there was just as much sitting and snogging and flirting, as there was actual bopping. The air was thick with smoke, as it generally was in pubs and clubs at the time. While it was exhilarating to finally find a lesbian hangout, it was, in reality, no place to meet anyone because the music drowned out most attempts at conversation. As I already had a girlfriend, I wasn't into picking anyone up. That first time I was more fascinated by watching a threesome, a butch woman in a dark suit, with a ribbon tie, and fascinatingly androgynous face, and her ultra-feminine girlfriend, who had an unexplained man, looking like a 1940s spiv, sitting close to her and who all three seemed entwined in some triangular scene incomprehensible to the rest of us, louche as a Toulouse Lautrec painting.

Another time, after a row with my girlfriend, I went to Caves on my own, intent on picking someone up, as that was clearly the main thing clubs were for. I got in somehow, probably by mentioning Pat, but as it was Sunday evening, the club was almost empty and the only woman open to conversation, Paddy, was plump, older, decidedly sloshed and slightly lugubrious. We agreed that it was not much of an night, and Paddy proposed relocating to the Longbranch, the one other lesbian club in Brighton at the time, at 75 Grand Parade, which I had heard was run by Peggy and her girlfriend Ros, one of whom was famously fierce on the door, but where I hoped to find someone more my own age. Paddy promised confidently that she could get me in, so off we went, by taxi, only to find that we were too late, and it was shut. I had to bribe a reluctant taxi driver to take the volubly drunken Paddy on home, while I thought better of wandering, and threaded my weary way back to Hove. I don't recall ever getting into the Longbranch, where I'm told photos of Martina Navratilova were fixed to the walls with drawing pins, until later on when the venue was reincarnated as the, equally gay, Pavilion Restaurant, with a distant view of the domes of Brighton Pavilion.

I did feel I was slightly taking my life in my hands every time I went to a lesbian club, because of my job, and being pretty sure that the head would not back me up if I was known to be gay. (I'm told by a friend who recalls Caves that she spotted wires poking through the Artex, and felt the risk to life there was more literal than struck me at the time.) It felt much safer going to monthly Kenric nights, which started up in 1985 at the Preston Park house of Rosemary Gascoyne, the artist, and her partner Lin, which, since you didn't even have to be a Kenric member to get in, were like parties with friends, where you would bring your own booze (and would stick to your own bottle), bop away among the huge abstract paintings in the front room, chat in the kitchen, put a pound in towards the French bread and cheese refreshments, and smoke wherever you liked. They became fancy dress parties every New Year's Eve, with ever more fabulous costumes, led by Rosemary's designer flair for transforming herself and Lin into Minnie and Micky Mouse, or Titania and Oberon. Those evenings cased altogether in 1992, when Rosemary and Lin moved to Scotland.

One other place I went to, soon after, the Sussex Club in Regency Square, was run by a pleasant straight couple. The woman, Shirley, with long blonde hair, was usually on the door, and I went there with two friends who have always been out as long as I have known them. We had to ring the bell, and when Shirley opened up, she asked me, 'What's your name?' and I turned to this couple and said, 'What is my name?' I couldn't remember what name I had used to sign in the last time! Shirley was amused, and let me in anyway. That was more spacious than Caves, large enough for a pool table, which was popular, and unlike Caves, had windows on to the square, which I don't think had the curtains drawn in daylight hours, so it felt more open.

Then there was Marilyn's, later renamed Harlequin's, in Providence Place, where women were welcome, though men were in the majority. Large enough to accommodate about 200 people, the big attraction there was the humour of the drag acts, all female impersonators, later on a Friday and Saturday night, and the dramatic central staircase, down which you could parade with your partner in your best going-out gear. Marilyn's was run by a very capable woman, short, plump and feminine, with curly hair, memorably described to me by a gay man as 'Maria with the big bazoongas'. Though a screaming success, it shut down suddenly and inexplicably, amid rumours of the owners falling out.

Different again were two explicitly feminist ventures of that decade in Brighton and Hove. They really were women-only: a departure from previous lesbian clubs I'd known where men were allowed in as guests. The longest surviving was The Only Alternative Left, at 39 St Aubyns, Hove, in a four-storey building, owned and managed by Monica Crowe. I always assumed she chose the name as a wry reaction to Thatcherism, at a time when so many progressive places and ideas were being decimated; but she said herself that she 'wanted it to be different to the usual pub and club everyone went to at that time. It was non-smoking, which was way ahead of its time.' [1]

TOAL originally opened as a women's vegetarian guesthouse on the upper floors in 1987, with self-service breakfasts in a small kitchen on the landing, and occasional long-term residents too. By 1990 Monica decided to open a women's bar on the ground floor, mainly on Fridays and Saturdays, which lasted out the whole decade, only closing in 2000, a long lifetime for a lesbian venue. It was a comfortable, stylish place, which felt more open than some of the clubs – you didn't have to sign in. It was just a pleasant place with ample space, where you could meet plenty of women. Some of my friends who had been to Rosemary and Lin's started going to Monica's instead, because it was somewhere where feminists felt welcome, among others, and it was easier to talk to people, because the music was in the background (dancing was confined to disco nights) and you could breathe free of smoke.

The ground floor bar was large and spacious, with sofas and soft chairs, and the smokers had to exit, either outside, or into an alcove screened off by heavy plastic curtains. (This compromise didn't go down well with

---

[1] Quoted on p.178 of *Queer in Brighton* (2014) edited by Maria Jastrzebska and Anthony Luvera (*New Writing South*)

some, in the decade before the law forced sociable smokers outside, for the good of everyone else's lungs.) You could also come for supper, and the first eatery there, the Purple Bat, was eventually replaced by Café Jules, a tasty vegetarian restaurant, run by Jules herself, on the first floor. While it was mainly frequented by lesbians, I did a double-take once when I walked in with my lover, and was warmly greeted by two straight councillors I knew from the Labour Party, an unexpected encounter between my different worlds, which I was keeping separate in order not to be outed at work.

Lesbian social life at The Only Alternative Left took diverse forms. One woman recalls 'a casino night where we all dressed glamorously and played roulette on a roulette wheel Monica had hired for the evening. There was at least one quiz night where every question had a lesbian theme. We gathered there to watch the 1990 TV drama *Portrait of a Marriage*. Sometimes it was a quiet evening and we'd play games like Connect 4 or Play on Wordz. Once a couple of us flipped a coin 50 times to see if would come up heads 25 times and tails 25 times. I bet it wouldn't, she bet it would. I won. There was a crimplene fancy dress evening where you had to come dressed in crimplene.'

The Only Alternative Left attracted the same broad range of women, gay and straight, as did the women's bookshops of the era, Sisterwrite and Silver Moon. While Caves felt edgy, TOAL felt safe. It even ran to teas in summer on a terrace in the garden. In the basement, a performance venue called the Well opened for a while. There were memorable evenings over the years with up and coming poet Jackie Kay. Performers also included, on various occasions, popular singers from the female circuit: Donna and Kebab (now known as Martha and Eve), Marianne Segal, Jan Allein, and the folksinger icon of my 1960s childhood TV viewing, Julie Felix. And all this without any membership fee – everything was pay-as-you-go and all women welcome, though it was overwhelmingly lesbian. Discos were separate, special, events, with an entrance fee: the main point of the place was conversation.

Not long after TOAL had opened, I arrived for one of the monthly Lesbian Line Socials. They had recently moved from the Regency pub, a mixed gay venue with flamboyant decor, created by a theatre set designer and his hairdresser boyfriend: hand-painted wallpaper, in dark green and pale green stripes; golden plaster cherubs and palm leaves; red velvet curtains; and a chandelier in the ladies' loo. When the Lesbian Line socials relocated to The Only Alternative Left, it was a complete change of ambience, with its single-colour plaster walls, soft modern seating, and images of and by women on the walls. I donated my poster of Sadie Lee's first National Portrait Gallery prize-winning portrait, of herself and her girlfriend, to Monica, which she hung in the bar. The Only Alternative Left surprised me by being so clean and spacious and comfortable, like the kind of straight hotel you might go to for a treat, rather than the cramped, dark, smoky gay spaces I was used to.

Standing in the queue for the bar at the Lesbian Line social, next to a shy-looking young woman, who looked vaguely familiar, I thought I should put her at her ease.

'Have we met here before? I think I know you from somewhere.'

'No, not here!' she said, very nervously. 'I've never been here before!'

'Oh, maybe it was at Rosemary's. Have you been there?'

'No!' she said, visibly uncomfortable. 'It was at college!'

'Oh my God, you're a student!' I said, and she explained that she had attended meetings of a lunchtime society I organised. I asked how she'd realised she was gay, and she said, she didn't know if she was, yet. It was hard to tell which of us was more terrified. 'I won't say anything if you don't!' And we neither of us did. And we each left the other well alone socially, apart from saying hello. It was the era of Section 28, and felt like the only safe thing to do. Section 28 only banned local authorities from 'the promotion of homosexuality', and not individual teachers, schools or colleges; liberal heterosexuals thought it as absurd as we did; and no prosecutions were brought under it. But it created a climate emboldening those who wanted to make life difficult for us, and, as ever, until 2003 you could be sacked, quite legally, for being lesbian, gay or bisexual. Happily, this young woman found her own way to a social circle and a relationship, and was even, I heard from friends, able to write a piece of Sociology coursework about coming out to her parents.

To the sorrow of all those who remembered her, Monica Crowe died of Covid in 2021, but thanks to her, people like this young woman had somewhere appealing to start out.

Closer to where I lived, another new women's club, the Blue Moon, a ground floor venue at 37 New England Road, was opened in the mid-1990s, by Shirley West, who lived in the flat upstairs with her partner. A mainstay of the Brighton Women's Centre, and key to their fundraising, Shirley had always wanted to open a club for lesbians, and actually made it happen, in the same way that Monica did, by owning a building and living on the premises. Both venues were a little out of the city centre: both women prioritised space over location, knowing that women would travel to meet up in welcoming venues.

Strong and stocky in build, Shirley West was practical, confident and capable, direct in speech, with a sardonic sense of humour: a really can-do woman who made things happen. Walking into the Blue Moon, you came straight into the bar, and through a doorway was a good-sized space for dancing and performance. Once, there was some amateur filming in the bar, which, in the 1990s, we still felt it a bit daring to appear in, but as we were all given a choice, and it was a lesbian filming, we weren't too bothered. Shirley's huge confidence and common sense that our sexuality was not a problem was infectious: we all felt a certain defiance about our right to live and thrive: and all the more, in reaction to Section 28, which glowered symbolically in the background of our youth from 1989 to 2003. In the 1980s and 1990s, I never took photos in lesbian clubs, or was photographed, unless it was between friends and we'd checked first that we had their permission. With the publication of *G-Scene* from 1995, a monthly gay and lesbian Brighton and Hove listings magazine (funded and edited by James Ledward) which started to feature photos of willing club-goers, things did become more relaxed over time. So appreciated was James Ledward, and so much did he donate to the LGBT+ community, that a new community centre, and a Brighton bus, have been named after him since his death in 2019, and *G-Scene* still survives, though recently renamed *Scene*.

One New Year's Eve, we put on a women's pantomime at the Blue Moon, directed by Carol Prior, who ran a local singing group. We had a lot of fun creating costumes Carol devised, with conical gold bras, based on the ones Madonna wore at the time. It was lesbian high camp, concocted with glue, cardboard, and satiny, glittery fabrics and sequins, with much laughter and everyone talking at once around the opened up, six-foot dining table in my basement sitting room. Carol's script was full of puns, to which we added, ad-libbing in rehearsals. The plot revolved around cowgirls, who were very in, due to the newish popularity of lesbian line dancing at the time, but the setting was rural Sussex. On the night, the event was packed out, and our slightly sexy, colourful and humorous production brought warm rounds of applause and whistling.

Sadly, despite Shirley urging us, like many a lesbian club owner before her, to use it or lose it, the Blue Moon only lasted about three years, as it wasn't financially viable enough to be worth continuing. While there is great theoretical affection for women's clubs in the lesbian community – the last nights at the legendary Gateways Club in Chelsea in 1985 were packed with women, some of whom had hardly been there for years – in reality, gay and bisexual women tend to frequent bars and clubs less than men do. Shirley sold off the contents, including some padded blue chairs which I acquired for £4 each, a memento of this bit of Brighton's lesbian history.

Very sadly, Shirley died suddenly, of natural causes, at the age of 56 in 2006. One of the movers and shakers of the lesbian community, she was a great loss to Brighton. As Treasurer she had played a key role in ensuring the Women's Centre found new premises and survived the threat of closure. Shirley West was one of those really out women, completely comfortable in her sexuality, an inspiration to those of us who were still more cautious about being out in every aspect of our lives.

My favourite lost places, however, were actually the bookshops of the era. Despite a few serendipitous discoveries in second-hand bookshops, like those then in St James Street, Kemptown, and Surrey Street, near Brighton Station, I felt starved of information in the early 1980s. I can still remember the huge excitement of discovering whole shelves of lesbian novels and non-fiction when my first girlfriend took me to Compendium, an alternative bookshop near Camden Lock Market. A smaller bookshop, with some lesbian stock, opened in Brighton in 1984, Read All About It in East Street. I also tried the radical Public House Bookshop in Preston Street (a yellow-fronted building that looked like the pub it had originally been) but, run by two men, that was stronger on Marxism than on lesbianism or feminism.

As I could find no women's bookshop or gay bookshop in Brighton or Hove, I graduated to Sisterwrite, the women's collective bookshop, at 190 Upper Street, Islington, and, when it opened in 1984, also to Silver Moon, the large women's bookshop in a prominent position in the heart of central London bookselling, at 64 Charing Cross Road (later 64-68). The appeal of the women's bookshops was partly the indefinite amount of time we were allowed to browse through all those books and magazines I never came across elsewhere, and the eventual prizes to which I would devote some of my limited budget. Among the highlights of my purchases were Rita Mae Brown's *Rubyfruit Jungle*, Angela Stewart-Park and Jules Cassidy's *We're Here: Conversations with lesbian women* and Isabel Miller's *Patience and Sarah*. Later on, the Lesbian History Group's *Not a Passing Phase*, Rosalind Pearson and Suzanne Neild's *Women Like Us* and Lilian Faderman's *Surpassing the Love of Men*, helped inspire me to research and write lesbian history myself.

But what was also magical was being in a space where lesbians felt at home, being welcomed among other women. Silver Moon was owned and run by two lesbians, Jane Cholmeley and Sue Butterworth, and there were lesbians among the collective at Sisterwrite. These felt like safe spaces for young women, wondering about their sexuality, to wander in to find out more, without feeling they were making a statement about being gay. While men were allowed in – Jim McSweeney (manager of Gay's the Word Bookshop) told me he once visited Silver Moon – the space was often filled by women. There was a huge lesbian section in the basement there, where you felt safely unobserved from the street. Noticeboards and leaflets made you feel connected to a community, and led you to other like-minded places and events. Affordable radical postcards, like those of Cath Tate, and arty, sometimes sexy, birthday cards of female couples, allowed you to impress and amuse your lover and your friends with unusual images. As women's presses were flourishing then, and republishing forgotten female classics, the books gave you a sense of connection to lesbians long gone from earlier eras. This is the sense of history that straight people get from their families, museums and film, in all of which lesbians felt largely absent to me until 1989, when *Out on Tuesday* was first screened on Channel 4, and *Oranges are not the Only Fruit* was first dramatised on BBC 2. There were also cafés in each bookshop, where you could meet up with friends, and book launches at Silver Moon could seat audiences of around 50, on the ground floor.

Not that size ever deterred bookshop owners. To our delight, Chris Farrah-Mills opened Out! Brighton, the only gay bookshop in the city, in 1994 at 4–7 Dorset Street, where book launches were originally held in the main bookshop section, with 25 or so of us squeezed in somehow, (and later moved to larger venues, like the Marlborough pub theatre). In the shop I often chatted to Chris, or his partner Rick, one of whom was often on the till, and found fascinating titles like Lynn Sutcliffe's *There Must Be Fifty Ways To Tell Your Mother* and James Gardiner's marvellous photo history of gay men, *Who's a Pretty Boy The*n? To help it survive, which it did till 2001, Out! also had a back room selling sex toys and erotic products, and like most radical bookshops, sold cards and badges, so that cash-strapped browsers still had some prize to carry home. Chris Farrah-Mills recalls that 'Out! Brighton was opened on World AIDS Day (1 December) 1994, by Peter Tatchell and featured on BBC2 Newsnight that evening. Out! was on TV nine times in all, was raided by homophobic youth seven times, had its windows smashed once, and was the scene of very many book launches. All Out! Staff were LGB and my time there was the happiest of my life.'

Once my own book launch had to be organised in 2003, absolutely all these bookshops had sadly closed down. Some were defeated by the ending of the net book price agreement which, until 1995, gave each book the same price, wherever it was sold. This used to protect independent bookshops from unfair competition, by avoiding the massive discounting we have today by book chains, supermarkets and online multinational companies. Often a sharp and impossible increase in the rent was the final straw for women's bookshops. Sisterwrite, which had been the first to open, in 1978, was the first to close, in 1993. Others that thrived, like Out!, faced growing competition, with the local Borders opening a huge LGBT book section, and Prowler and Clone Zone launching in St James Street. As Chris Farrah-Mills recalls, 'Many of the small radical presses have closed down because the big stores wanted more discount than they were able to provide.'

When Silver Moon shut in 2001, after 17 years trading, the brand was cannily sold to Foyles, in whose Silver Moon department Pandora Press launched my book *From the Closet to the Screen: Women at the Gateways Club 1945-85*, in 2003. As I was reading to the packed room, where all seats were taken, and it was standing room only, I spotted one of my many interviewees, Susannah York, creeping discreetly into the back row, and giving me a big smile of encouragement. How far I had come since, as a closeted young student, I had first seen Susannah on screen, in *The Killing of Sister George*. After the flurry of eager women had had their books signed, Maggi Hambling enticed several of us, including Maureen Duffy, her partner and me, off to the drag show at Molly Moggs, the Soho pub just down the street.

Sadly, a year later, even this remnant of Silver Moon had vanished too. Now, even Molly Moggs has closed. My loyalties have since transferred to the ever-resilient Gay's the Word, surviving against all the odds since 1979, at 66 Marchmont Street, Bloomsbury, where I was able to hold one of the launches for my latest book *With Some Wild Woman: Poems 1989–2019*. Kenric is still flourishing, showing that for the women's scene, networks are key, not bricks and mortar businesses. I did find other women's clubs later on: notably the Glass Bar, run by Elaine McKenzie, marvellously located in a discreet two-storey tower, outside Euston Station. And there were various incarnations of the Candy Bar: one in Soho, but another in Brighton, located underground at first, before it moved to a boldly open shop-windowed ground floor space, in St James Street, leaving the basement space to a new mixed club called Zanzibar. The clubs I knew are all closed now. Yet whatever places are lost, someone is always starting a new one, as the emergence of the Feminist Bookshop in Brighton showed, in 2019, which is LGBTQ+-friendly. And Meet Up gives you all the social life you could wish for. Occasional lesbian disco nights survive, wherever the space is suitable.

For my birthday parties and book launches, I rely today on hiring private rooms in gay-friendly venues, like the Phoenix Artists Club, which regularly hosted the Incite LGBT poetry nights, just up the road from where Silver Moon was. The sheer presence of lesbians in the majority creates that comfortable vibe we cannot always find reliably elsewhere, a place where we are not 'othered', or expected to explain our choices, and can simply relax, be ourselves and let our hair down. That's how we survived.

The Carved Red Lion – 2 Essex Road Islington, London circa 1980
Gary McGhee

It was the best of times and the worst of times. Unfortunately part of the latter was the state of the 'gay scene' in London in the late 70s. Me and my radical, left-wing friends bemoaned the lack of alternatives to an increasingly commercialised scene that was dominated by FriscoDisco, US-import clones, dance round your handbag pop and Hi-Energy pap (as we saw it). We were gay and lesbian punks, rockabillies, skinheads, post-punks, goths, (before that tribe had been established), trannies and he-dykes and had clothes, musical tastes, and attitudes to match. We were alienated from a straight society which kept us illegal until we were 21 (I was 19) and raided our spaces and arrested us and sent out pretty policemen to entrap us in cottages. Being out at work was generally fraught with hassle and homophobic discrimination. We might as well have been living in the 50s. So, a loosely-linked network of friends decided to do something about it and set up a gay night in a venue that would play our music, reflect our politics, be somewhere that people like us could dance and be safe-ish. One night that could be ours. That was the theory anyway. So a gay Marxist collective that produced a magazine called *Gay Noise*, which I was involved with at the time (now that's another story), approached a bar in Islington, which was fast becoming a centre of gay radicalism, and got the landlord to agree to a trial run of Saturday nights. Obviously, he wanted to get more punters in to buy beer. No problem there. So, with the use of the basement bar, which had a modestly sized dancefloor, we set up what became a legendary and literally underground, alternative gay night. The also legendary DJs Bernie and Martin spun the discs and had immaculate taste in post-punk tunes and grooves. (They took up residency for many years as DJs at the Bell in King's Cross after that.) So, what was it like? It was dark, dank, sweaty, claustrophobic, and utterly fantastic, unique, new, vibrant, truly a sub-subcultural revolution, and it was cheap. It quickly built up in reputation and numbers and became the go-to place for a year or so. I had many memorable nights there, and met many new like-minded friends, and lovers as well as those I already knew. One of those, who went on to become a famous Scottish popstar, would approach the odd straight voyeurs who managed to wangle their way in and tell them to 'get the fuck out, this is a gay night, you have the whole fucking world to go dancing in' etc. We had to restrain him before he gave them a Glasgey kiss. (You can take the Boy out of Glasgey but you can't take the Glasgey out of the boy...) Another night we got raided by Rugby fans from Leeds. Their girlfriends had ventured down the stairs, intrigued by the music, and when I told them it was a gay night (I was on the door at the time), informed me that their boyfriends wouldn't like that. No shit, Sherlock. Right on cue their boyfriends, about 10 of them, came down the stairs, so I had to call for reinforcements from the bar and about 10 of us blocked the way in. The police were called and dispersed the Leeds neds and nedesses, but also made us turn the music off, and end the night. After a few more incidents later the landlord decided that we were more trouble than we were worth, so the operation was forced to decant to the Pied Bull round the corner. This soon got raided by fascist skinheads (the neds were preferable) and the police did nothing when they attacked us as we left, but that is another story. Those were the days. The best of times and the worst of times. The CRL basement did continue to be a lesbian bar for some time after, but it is now a pub called The Winchester. The Bell took over as 'ourspace', but it will always be fondly remembered as a pioneering entity, that was a blast while it lasted.

Clapham Common Diary
John Dixon

Clapham Common is triangular. Near its acute angle is an elongated triangle of trees and bushes. This is the trolling area. Many towns and parks have such places. I came across this one by chance, and soon became a devotee. I was keeping a diary at that time and a day's entry – after topics such as work, socialising, holiday, theatre-going etc – often rounded off with goings-on 'over the Common'.

Two days a week I finished work at 8pm and did not get home till 9.30 or so. I didn't object to the travel; I rather liked a good distance between work and home life. An evening stroll, across the Common, sitting on a bench, a cigarette or two, reflecting on the day's events, was a great unwind. It often led to an unbutton, unbuckle and unzip.

The Common never has been much to look at by day; laid-out sports pitches, a few avenues of trees, a bandstand at the cross-road of paths, a couple of ponds surrounded by rushes. But by night you realised how open it was, on quite a high plateau, the sides dipping away, and the stars – doubtless an illusion – seeming clearer. The noise of the traffic was muted. Fewer people were around – dog-walkers, joggers, strollers – all far friendlier than by day.

Under the trees there was an even greater thinning out. People were there for one reason only. No justifications, no formal introductions, no speech necessary. The paths were well-trodden, the off-shoots easily explored. I learned to avoid the exposed roots, and the areas that often became water-logged. I lost any fears that a rustling in the bushes might spell danger. The haunt almost assumed the 'form' of a retreat or magic garden, always worth a visit, even without any intent of doing anything.

Of course, I listened to the various scare stories, but never worried too much about police harassment or muggers, or about moral clean-up vigilantes concerned about their children or house-prices. It was too early to be paralysed inactive by the growing threat of AIDS. Perhaps I took the place too much for granted and assumed the escape, the idyll would never end.

Well, not end. Taper off. It was not that I was caught in flagrante, had to appear in court, be sentenced, shamed, move house and still live in fear of exposure. Not that I was hospitalised after a mugging. Not even – which was true – that I had got a job nearer to home, and the reassuring separation of work and home life no longer applied. What put me off, dampened my enthusiasm, was the unexpected, sudden impact on the night of 15–16 October 1987 of The Great Storm.

It was not the fear of God, divine retribution, but the ruination of a familiar territory. The transformation of something certain and reachable into something alien and distant.

I didn't choose to visit the Common the day immediately after the storm. I left it a couple of days and went by day on a sad reconnoitre. The approach avenue had uprooted trees, and left huge gaps like knocked-out teeth. In the trolling area the usual paths were more than ever waterlogged. Access was denied by fallen trees, collapsed into one another. Upturned branches seemed almost to be rooting themselves. The little enclaves, favourite trees, hideaways, overhangs of bushes and creeper, had been torn apart, like a canopy dismembered.

Things got back to a kind of normal. The area dried out, people started trysting again. I couldn't get the measure of the new layout. My feet had lost auto-pilot. Familiar things dragged out of shape may have their own fascination, but I still tried to re-imagine how it once had been. I became obsessed with the memories of each fallen tree. The one I often leaned against while a faceless supplicant, on his knees, head-bobbing, plied his trade. Or my face to the tree-trunk as if doing hamstring extension exercises and trying to keep my balance while being pumped into. Or in the other role when I desperately embraced both man and tree-trunk and tried to maintain my balance on the slippery earth round the tree base. To each tree its episode.

The Council cleared away some fallen trees. In some cases the main branches were removed and the trunk left. The undergrowth was thinned out and saplings were planted that would never grow to any size. Later benches and litters bins were added. The benches were never inscribed with any memorable dedications. I remember one bench on Hampstead Heath with the wording 'In memory of … … who loved strolling in these woods.' I always wanted to fill in the first S, 'who loved trolling in these woods.' The litter bins never succeeded in gathering to their bosom their intended, the condoms, tissues and poppers bottles.

Latterly the Friends of Clapham Common put up a plaque filling in the historical details and what you could expect to find. 'You are now standing in Battersea Woods.' I'd never heard the trolling area called that. There were also details for flora. 'The woods contain fine examples of Black Elder and False Acacia.' These, after years of visiting, had missed my scrutiny. There was no mention of fauna. Nor the nightlife who used to come from miles around to enjoy the woods, and become shades, zombies and the spirits of the place.

I mentioned to a writers' group I belonged to that I was thinking of publishing extracts from my diary, especially the trolling episodes. Anyone included would be unnamed, and very possibly dead or at least changed beyond recognition. The account might even serve as some sort of historical record, and could be used as a comparison with the current situation.

A new member of the writing group was enthusiastic. He was from Europe, the first country to legalise same-sex marriage. He claimed he was eager to learn about the history of backward gay customs in this country. He asked if I would show him round the trolling area. Which I did one fine midday.

The area never looks its best by day and he was shocked. He said in a voice with suppressed emotion

'So! THIS is where those poor people were forced to come to meet others. They had no other outlet. It was not their fault!' He made a despairing gesture. Well, I thought, the trolling area may not be one of the world's greatest arboreta ... but ... of a moonlit midnight ... 'Thank God,' he continued, 'things have changed. And there are now so many, many other ways to meet people without resorting to a place such as THIS. THOSE days are over.' He gave an expansive, all-encompassing gesture ending in a dismissive flick of the wrist. 'THIS is of the past.'

He thanked me profusely for bringing him there. 'I have seen for myself. I know now what suffering and privations you must have had to put up with in those days.' He gave me a reassuring pat, as if to say 'All over now. All over.'

Like many people gripped by lofty and evangelistic ardour he failed to notice the world immediately around him. He certainly missed a tissue here and a tissue there. And not a few inches from his feet, tucked under a tuft of grass, was a used condom, shit-flecked.

John Dixon, *A Common Pursuit*; the trolling diaries, is due for publication shortly.

Gay Galleries Gone
Jeffrey Doorn

In considering lost LGBT places, we may wistfully or ruefully remember pubs, clubs, cruising grounds, cottages and related venues. While those are all important, I can't help thinking of the lovely little art galleries I've known, those quirky queer spaces where one could enjoy displays of male nudity in a quasi-respectable context.

Apparently, the Ebury Gallery, at 89 Ebury Street in Belgravia, specialised in male or queer art in the early 1980s, showing Mark Wardell and others I discovered later. I did not know of this venue at the time; any information or memories of it would be welcome.

I can't quite recall exactly when or how I discovered St Jude's; it must have been around the time it first opened, at 107 Kensington Church Street, in the mid-1980s. Philip Graham and Stephen Boyd, partners in life and business, were the curators and art dealers who set up and ran the small shop. They regularly staged exhibitions by artists both well-established and up-and-coming. One month, visitors would be treated to sketches from life by Cecil Beaton or drawings by Keith Vaughan; another time we would see recent sensual works by Cornelius McCarthy or romantic watercolours by Myles Antony.

While the nude male form predominated, it was not the only subject. David Hutter's output, for example, included flower paintings and landscapes; while Peter

Samuelson featured fully-clothed young men, often in domestic settings. Proceeds from the latter's July 1989 show, 'Recent Friends' went to AIDS charities. Village and city scenes by post-impressionist René Pirola (1872-1912) were also shown in 1989, as were Kevin Whatney's Australian Images, from Great Barrier Reef flora and fauna to surfers and athletes.

Other artists on display included Alain Rosello, John Vere Brown, Gavin Maughfling, Alan Halliday with drawings of dancers and athletes, and Lin Jammet, Elisabeth Frink's son, whose first London exhibition was at the gallery in May 1990, with another the following year. Annual exhibitions of The Male Nude and Christmas shows gathered paintings, drawings and prints by groups of artists such as I. D. Baker, Peter Forster, Martin Ireland, Ilric Shetland, Diccon Swan and Kevin Whitney.

St Jude's also sold books, e.g. Hutter's 1984 collection *Nudes and Flowers*, and the 1989 publication *Life Class: The Academic Male Nude 1820–1920*, edited by Boyd with an introduction by Edward Lucie-Smith, and hosted book launches, e.g. autumn 1990 publications by Gay Men's Press. Philip and Stephen edited numerous catalogues and books, notably *Keith Vaughan 1912–1977: Drawings of the Young Male*, published to coincide with an exhibition in the gallery May–June 1991 and reissued in paperback by GMP in 1994.

Private views launching each show were enjoyable social affairs, and one got to know not only the artists on display but also the art lovers and collectors who gathered together to view and perhaps purchase.

The gallery's final year brought Singapore artist Yeo

Kim Seng, American Emlan Etting (1905–93) and an intriguing show, 'The Male Nude, The Woman's View' featuring works in different media by twelve artists including Frink, Inge Clayton, Sandra Fisher with seductive pastels and charcoal drawings, Jacqueline Morreau, Mireille Spademan and sculpture by Jill Tweed.

Sadly, St Jude's closed at Christmas 1991. Regular customers were aware that Stephen was very ill and were concerned for his health; word went round that he had AIDS. Philip carried on, opening a new, much larger gallery, as Philip Graham Contemporary Art, initially joined by Stephen, at 9a–11 Bonhill Street, between Old Street and Moorgate. There he displayed the familiar stable of artists, plus works by many others, e.g. Stuart Bullen, Ian Gardner, Geoff Woodhead, studies by William Edward Frost (1810–77) and a retrospective of Philip Osborne (1926–94) with a range of imagined characters full of desire and tenderness. I acquired a lovely head and shoulders study by Philip Core, American born artist and writer based in London, who had died aged 38 in 1989, another AIDS victim. Stephen died in 1993; Philip succumbed in 1995, aged 49.

Occasionally a general art gallery would feature an artist previously seen at St Jude's. In 1991, Roy Miles Gallery at 29 Bruton Street held an exhibition celebrating Peter Samuelson in his 80th year, five years before his death. With the loss of Philip's Bonhill Street gallery, one searched for similar showings of familiar artists.

Feeling bereft of a specialist venue for depictions of the male form, I was delighted to discover Adonis Art in 1998. At 1b Coleherne Road, just around the corner from the long-established gay pub, Adonis boasted a ground floor shop, with a changing display of paintings in the windows and a wealth of artworks within. Pictures ranging from 19th century academic studies to current pieces in varied media, sculpture, postcards and greeting cards were on offer.

Exhibitions were held down in the basement, opening to a little courtyard where drinks were served during private views. The first show I attended was 'Treasures of the Night', a retrospective of paintings by Matthew Stradling, beautiful bodies in pearl-encrusted fantasy settings. He returned with new works in 2002 and 2005.

Some of the former St Jude's artists became regulars at Adonis, in particular Myles Antony, whose soft-focussed scenes proved perennially popular. I found him charming to chat with and was delighted to meet some of his pretty models. Other familiar names included Martin Ireland, Peter Samuelson in posthumous shows and Cornelius McCarthy, with an exciting display of 'Beach Bodies' in 2004, new paintings shortly before his death in 2009 and memorial exhibitions in following years.

Hugh Sowden had exhibited in several London galleries, including Cork Street in the 1970s, before relocating to Egypt in 1981; there he created many works, notably frescos for All Saints Cathedral, Cairo. Adonis welcomed his return to UK with 'Idylls & Instincts: Paintings from Egypt' in June 2004.

Several artists were shown time and again, so patrons could follow their development: George Cayford, Andrew Potter, Mike Thorn, Yuliang Wu, Philip Swarbrick, David Thompson, David Ambrose and Nebojsa

Zdravkovic to name a few. Works by these and others ranged from Swarbrick's glistening gladiators and alley boys to Thorn's bear art, edgy urban scenes, shadowy domestic settings, sunshine and sea views or fetish photography. There were also summer and Christmas group shows and sales from patrons' collections.

Special events included Edward Lucie-Smith signing his book *Flesh and Stone* and a life class to have a go at drawing a nude model in various poses. Customers meeting at private views came to recognise each other, discussing the work on show and forming friendships. Sometimes conversations continued at the Coleherne, which had been transformed from a homely gay pub to a glitzy venue with stainless steel decor. Since then, as we know, it has become a straight gastro-pub, renamed The Pembroke.

Adonis Gallery closed in March 2013 when the lease ran out and proved too expensive to renew. Proprietor Stewart Hardman, who had already been selling artworks online, moved the business to the Internet, initially sending out an email newsletter to former patrons and referring customers to his website. Viewing works of art this way is, of course, not the same as experiencing them in the flesh, seeing the brushstrokes, texture, patina etc. It was possible to view by appointment at Stewart's home; I never availed myself of that opportunity. A recent online search indicates Stewart has now moved to Manchester, and Adonis Art International remains an online service. It is good that Adonis hasn't faded out entirely; but I do miss the buzz of entering the shop, chatting with Stewart, descending the stairs to exhibitions and enjoying them with a glass of wine while socialising with other art lovers.

Queer art shows do appear in different locations from time to time, and the annual Loudest Whispers exhibition features LGBT artists for February's History Month, at St Pancras Hospital or the Old Diorama Arts Centre NW1; but there is no dedicated gallery for such work.

Celebrating the male form, Henry Miller Fine Art exhibited regularly at Coningsby Gallery, Tottenham Street for a number of years. Miller also held open house viewings at his home in Walthamstow by invitation to mailing-list members, becoming strictly limited under Covid-19 restrictions, then suspended during lockdowns. With such restrictions ended, occasional exhibitions and open house viewings have resumed. These showings are very welcome; but one hopes that someday we will again have a shop front gallery with a rolling programme of exhibitions to enjoy year round.

112 JEFFREY DOORN

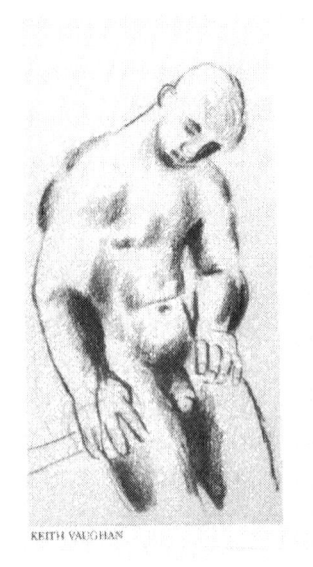

Keith Vaughan drawing (St Jude's third annual exhibition of the Male Nude) and David Hutter 'October' (St Jude's, a 1981 painting used in the book Nudes and Flowers, *GMP 1984)*

John Vere Brown painting (St Jude's March/April 1990)

GAY GALLERIES GONE 113

Lin Jammet first exhibition (St Jude's May 1990)

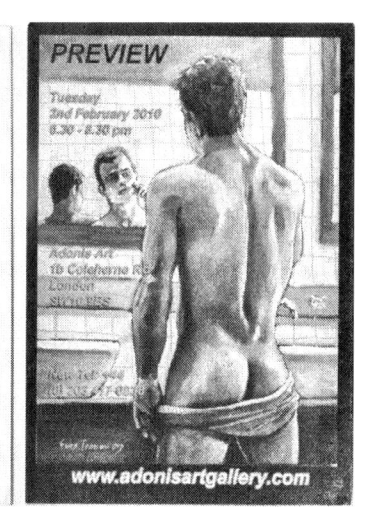

'Treasures of the Night' (Adonis September 1998) and Adonis Preview February 2010 (image by Gena Ivanov)

*'Post-War Friends Revisited' by Peter Samuelson,
shown at Adonis in 2009*

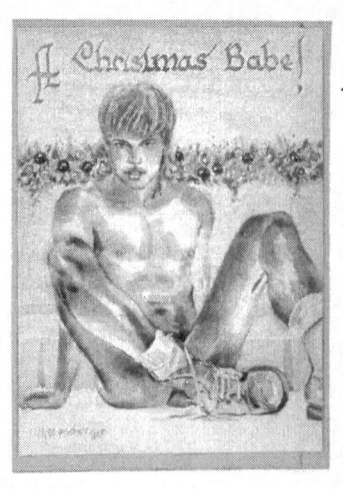

*Adonis Christmas Fair 2000 invitation
(with image by Myles Antony)*

Out and Down in London and Paris
David Flybury

I can't imagine men and women liking each other the way men like each other. I can't imagine men and women touching each other the way men touch each other. After all, why would they? So, I'm queer! and there's an end to it.

***

You can't just live with your parents. You have to go out and live in the big wide world. In 1984 due to my own machinations and those of circumstance, I found myself with a gaping hole where my future should have been; I was alone in London, and 21, and, I suppose, I was in pursuit of the hedonistic lifestyle the epicentre of which I imagined to be Heaven nightclub underneath Charing Cross station. Nevertheless my perambulations took me more frequently to El Sombrero on Kings Road, a single subterranean room sectioned into three – an elevated bar area across one corner, a dance floor opposite, and a cruise area in between. I can't remember much else except that one night I went home with a glossy-haired Sri Lankan because I thought he had bought me a drink. He hadn't. My friend Jose had. Jose was manager of the insanely camp 'Reflections' restaurant across the road. Reflections restaurant had a tree-sized artificial tree in the middle of the room which they dressed in green leaves or flowers or brown leaves or snow: It 'reflected' the seasons, geddit? I usually went there earlier in the evening to pose. It suited them to have youth flouncing round the bar. Jose would prep me with free vodka before the rigours of the evening ahead. I smoked long brown cigarettes flavoured with menthol ('Mores') and wore silk shirts that were several sizes too big – I picked those up from the market at Camden Lock for a fiver. But to be honest I don't remember those times with much affection. I was on my uppers and wondered if I had what it took to be a prostitute. Nervous times. I briefly dated a banker who lived in Hampstead. I met him in the Salisbury – which just about sums the situation up.

But I already knew that true gay life, the real gay life was at that time in Europe and most specifically in the bars and *boîtes de nuit*, les caveaux de Paris (before le Marais or east Paris scene developed). Le Scaramouche (le Scara) near to the Paris Bourse was my favourite, closely followed by BH, Broad, Le Sept, le Dix-Huit, Duplex bar (still there), and the classically titled Limelight Boys International – all variously close to the brand new Les Halles complex (which has since been replaced). I knew all their names. I knew all their characters. You could get in for free on weekdays. One night Le Scara gave free drinks if you wore shorts. So I did.

My friend Paul did as well – his nylon green shorts still alive in my memory; we hid down a stairwell to the parking underneath the Bourse to change out of our jeans, and danced all night long to Hazel Dean and Marsha Raven – one had a song called 'Searchin' (lookin' for love)' and the other had a song called 'Catch me (I'm fallin' in love)', and I never could tell them apart.

We left with the sunrise.

Courtesy of a friend, Paul had a studio apartment behind La Samaritaine, Pont Neuf, between the Louvre and Rue de la Monnaie; it is still a site of pilgrimage for me, decades later. The bed, up on a makeshift mezzanine (like a duplex, Paul quipped) left no room to kneel, or anything: I hit my head; Paul got cramp in his leg and yelped, but laughed – incomprehensibly to me – when I, wanting to say, 'What is it?' translated this as, 'Qu'est-ce que c'est?'

'It is a leg!', he said, vastly amused.

My French was useless!

These clubs, more often than not, had enormous mirrored walls where cute boys in tight jeans would pose and dance, it seemed interminably, with themselves. On Thursdays Le Scara put on a show: Around 1 a.m. all the boys were cleared and blankets and pillows thrown down on the shiny steel floor; we sat and cheered as the stage illuminated and various talented drag queens took turns mimicking the greatest torch-bearers history had at that moment provided us with: Piaf regretting rien, Dalida sur scène. It was magic! The acts would banter with the boys on the front row of the audience speaking too quickly for me to understand, but I was trans-fixed, you might say; I remember one boy kneeling up and excitedly pointing to his mate, shouting, 'Lui – il suce bien!' – which means, 'his French is excellent!' And everyone (everyone) agreed!

Le BH was known as a raunch club – a kind of fey, Parisian Coleherne – filled with leather queens. 'Faux-macho'. But am I wrong to remember its dance floor as a disorientating cuboid room the floors, ceilings and walls of which were identically clad in white glass? Coloured disco lights flickered through, flashing it seemed never quite in time with the music. This hermetic luminous box was broken only by a spiral staircase from the bar above, descending out of a circular hole cut in the ceiling, and a gloomy, aquarium-like window, behind which the DJ rocked his cans in diode-illuminated darkness. And dancing there one night, all alone, like a moth caught in Tupperware – did I dream that?

I am definitely right to recall one Sunday afternoon stumbling into Le Broad, lit only by the brilliant afternoon sun filtering in through half closed doors; its two-level basement-and-mezzanine dance-floor was packed with boys who all seemed to be my age, or roughly, and I remember thinking, 'Everyone here is gay! Everyone, like me! Everyone, theoretically available!' We were Big in Japan! We were Alphaville! And suddenly it wasn't strange; it was unbelievable! They might fancy me and I might fancy them and they might fancy each other!

Coming back to London was like returning to prison. They were pretty desperate times. I had a job at the mega-Sainsbury's on Cromwell Road. That paid for it. I don't remember eating much. My money went on clubs and drinks and poppers. Youth is strange; you want to live in the night; I was still looking for my 'hedonistic lifestyle', I suppose. Was I looking for someone to love me? I suppose I was. We all are, after all, looking for someone to love.

***

The back room in the Salisbury theatre pub in St. Martin's

Lane consisted (and I assume still does) of walls of mirrors mounted in gilt ornamented frames in the highly opulent style of the late Victorians. Beneath the mirrors a long bench went right round the room with two gaps, one for a door which led into the street and another for the door which led into the front bar. The bar was highly mixed but the backroom was ours, solidly queer, wall to wall. The first time I went there I took my half-pint into the backroom and found a gap on the bench. There was a small table where I put my drink. It sounds like I knew what I was doing. A guy squeezed down next to me. He was my age. Danny. When we left he took me to a mews entrance nearby and pointed to a staircase that led down below ground. 'I'll go first; you follow,' he murmured. So I did. As I descended into the darkness I heard his voice again. I followed it. We fucked. He gave me his address and when I turned up on his doorstep in South Ken some time later, he gave me a bed and I stayed several months. It became a pattern. I was essentially homeless in this way for the next few years.

Not so long after our, erm, brief encounter, the Salisbury was cleared of its gay clientele by determined and rather brusque bouncers. They knew who to push off and, as far as I know, the Salisbury has been straight ever since.

But Danny was a good guy (with an amazing collection of super-tiny underpants) and like all the lost gay faces, I wonder what became of him. I hope that, as I did, he found some sort of love.

The Salisbury was old school queer full of lots of old school rent – boys who mixed an eagerness for sex with a willingness to accept generosity. I certainly accepted my fair share of generosity – though the guys with whom I was having sex weren't always the ones providing the generosity. I'm not sure the dive bar that the Salisbury was replaced by ('Brief Encounter' opening just across the road in 1985) had significantly different clientele though its style was quite different. Dark and modern, it could be more blatantly cruisy because, A, it was underground and, B, the times they were a-changing; the gay scene in London was burgeoning with a sudden burst of confident investment: 'First Out' café opened near Centre Point and was immediately packed with a newly self-confident crowd of radicalised gays and lesbians. You had to queue to get in, and it only sold coffee! Soon after that, 'Village' in Hanway Street, another underground café-bar, was so popular the crowds queued back into Oxford Street. I chased this rent-a-queue (which means something different in French) as it swept on to each new venue until there were so many places to go the crowd wore itself out: 'Crews' (all puns intended), on Upper St Martin's Lane was just about the last of that particular flood-tide. It had spectacular go-go boys who stood up on the long bar to gyrate, so there was always something nice to look at. That was in the 90s. When I went there there was always someone I knew; Wayne and Alva, for example, who introduced me to this cute Andrzej character who liked to dance as much as I did – he was a Polish visitor following on from the collapse of the Berlin Wall, and, 20 years later, my husband.

My last memory of Briefs, as we called Brief Encounter, is also from the 90s when I went there with my friend

Mark to see-in the New Year. We stood casually drinking and chatting and cruising in the rather small, extremely tightly packed room downstairs until the moment of countdown was announced. Simultaneously, everybody realised that in a very short while the man they were standing next to might be the one they would have to kiss to bring in the New Year – and they didn't want to kiss 'that'! Everybody wanted someone else. Someone ideal. Someone better. I was standing next to Mark, of course, but I didn't want to kiss a friend; I wanted to kiss a lov-err-maan! So we all decided at once to move to a different part of the room, a better place, somewhere the pickings were supposedly much richer: towards that bloke on the other side of the strobe-darkness we had been fancying all evening. As a result, the hive-mind of gay bodies self-organised into a gradually speeding vortex as each one of us tried to break free of our fate and find, in a few seconds, the one great love, or snog, of our life, or night. The plan was self-defeating. Churning madly when the clock struck we all found ourselves standing next to the very same people we had been trying to avoid – and instead of going for it with polite resignation or feigned enthusiasm, as the bongs of Big Ben passed damply, everyone looked down at their shuffling feet. It was an ignominious moment in gay history and, I assume, not elsewhere recorded.

***

The Paris of those years is as lost as that London, but when I heard about the death of Le Scara it was my own indifference that shocked me. Had I moved on or had I simply given up on the dreams and excitements its hallowed walls had once contained? Well, the truth is, I had moved on, obviously! My perambulations had taken me to a meticulous exploration of Paris's gay saunas: The 'Grand Sauna de l'Opéra', Rue du 4 Septembre, close by Garnier's concoction, replicated the imagined appearance of what a vast underground gay sauna would have been had it been built by the Romans – saucy mosaic, Corinthian columns everywhere, faux-marble bar, fancy restaurant, a beautiful pool and all the facilities for a total re-enactment of Caligula's most notorious excesses – minus (I'm pretty sure) the horses. Meanwhile, over on the Boulevard Montmartre, the IDM (say 'LiDi-em') was a less pretentious, I mean more blatantly earthy take on the same theme. Perhaps more Byzantine than Roman, the cavernous and labyrinthine IDM is one gay haunt still going strong, catering as it does to the raw sex act in a way the Internet never can. Other saunas were smaller and had their own themes. The unglamorous Tilsitt, famously, was for older men (not rent); Key West (still open) was for youth. A chacun son goût, as they say.

In the early 1980s Paris was very much 'l'endroit gai du monde'. The first phrase I learned was the liberating, 'Je m'en fous!' – kindly translated to me as, 'Frankly my dear I don't give a damn!' Gay Freedom had been, it seems, historically conditioned into the Parisian soul, with its Follies Bergère high-kicks take on public morality; a post-WWII enthusiasm for erasure and newness; the residual delirium of the Georges Pompidou-era disco-slash-Pierre Cardin aesthetic; and finally the dirigiste efflorescence of François Mitterand's Grand-Projet leftist-capitalism. Paris was optimistic and liberated and just simply better than anywhere else (even le Métro Parisien was beautiful).

(Though I should note that Paris was no bed of roses either. Once, when Paul and I were at Le BH, he introduced me to a friend of his, an older man. Later, Paul fixed me with his eye and said with chilling seriousness, boggling my mind at the destitutions he was leaving undescribed, 'I have had to do horrible things. Horrible things.' I, who was inveterately unserious and sexually obsessed, thought this unfeasibly cute. He pouted his lips sorrowfully. He was so sweet. Where is he? 'Disparue,' as the song says, 'tu as disparue...')

London at that time, in contrast, berated itself for all of history's failings: the failure of the imperial project; the failure of the socialist project; the failure of the capitalist project; and now the failure of the project of sexual and societal liberation (ultimately signalled by the censorious and hatred-promoting Section 28 of the Local Government Act, 1988 – which you might care to look up, Monsieur Internet): Nothing had worked and, with the so-called, 'Winter of Discontent', nobody worked either. All around, this sense of exhausted collapse permeated even those who took it upon themselves to attempt a rebuilding of what once had been – in so many different ways – a soi-disant New Jerusalem. This appalling mood of failure mixed with anger made London an exciting place to be – you either thrilled to the fact that the rapine Vandals were at the gate, or exalted brutishly that you were one of the Vandals. Thatcherite Britain had its own peculiar heroism, but it was not a fun place to be gay, particularly if your idea of being gay was, like mine, hedonistic and dissipatory! Throughout the 80s and into the 90s I took the train, boat, hovercraft, hydrofoil, plane, Eurostar (from November 14, 1994) or whatever, whenever I could, to get to gay Paris.

***

One night in a club in Les Halles – I don't remember which one; it wasn't Limelight Boys International! – a guy approached me and said he had seen me earlier, in another dive up the road, and had been following me. I took this stalking as a compliment. He was tall and ugly – features I always found encouraging – and very French. It is easy to think you know who to trust; so when he asked me back to his place, I went along, and when he said it was a bit of a journey I said, 'ok!' Even though I was leaving for London the next day, I didn't really think twice when we boarded a train, transferring from the RER to SNCF. Some time later we were at his place, a glass fronted gaff in a quiet street christ knows where. Inside … well I don't remember the details but I do remember … his cock, which was in the French tradition: absolutely huge. We wanted to fuck, naturally, and were getting to it except that … I didn't think I could – which, for me, really was saying something! – and he said he didn't have any lubricant as though he had never previously needed any; which, you can imagine, I was surprised to hear.

The complexities of condom usage might have been part of the problem; though I don't remember it, this was, after all's said and done, the 80s and the terror of AIDS was never far from one's mind. However louche the impression my tale might be giving, we all, all of us, spent many, many nights in sweaty fear of seroconversion, checking our necks for swollen glands, rehearsing our obituaries, planning our final months.

I mean, apologies to Bertolucci but this actually happened: 'I think I have some butter,' he said after an initial attempt, 'in the fridge.' Au frigo; I declined the offer. He resorted to spit. I waited and then … Well, afterwards he said, 'That would have been better if I'd had some lubricant.' D'uuh. Perhaps he had expected me to provide my own – and I would've, if I'd known! A little later, I phoned my friend Michel, with whom I was staying, in Paris 10ème, to say that I would be back in time to catch my train from Gare du Nord; turns out, I was in Orléans – which (you might not know this) is some 140km/90minutes south of Paris! I didn't know anything! – and what shocks me, in retrospect, is that I didn't care. Though, what shocks me more is that he didn't have any lubricant. And what shocks me even more is that I didn't care. But what shocks me most of all is that I didn't get his phone number.

***

Paris seemed to permit me to be myself. Back in London, I was like some boring exile, and insisted on deploying my painfully inadequate French in inappropriate and pretentious gobbets whenever I could – '… et riant la nuit!' – a Florence Foster Jenkins of that most cultivated tongue. I remember once giving my weary assent to unwelcome sex (round the corner from Portland Place) with the words, 'Comme tu veux …' (what a withering phrase; not that it dissuaded him!) (thank goodness). Ah, the tyranny of my foolishness ... but those nights drifting round Les Halles had become archetypal to me of a lifestyle with which I was now obsessed.

Dreams are like currents that flow and eddy, retracing our memories with imperfect repetition; for years and years afterwards, living in London, I dreamed myself into a series of backstreet clubs and hangouts that had never existed, picking up boys I had never known, in a fictional Paris I had never visited; dreaming it all, its utter familiarity, their velvet skin, soft and tan, and ... everything about them – waking to sense in that momentary angst of recollection once again all the glorious joy of those lost gay places, those lost gay faces, and my

sweet yearning.

Les infos:
www.goodbyelondontown.wordpress.com

Les chansons:

'Disparue', Jean-Pierre Mader, 1985　youtu.be/rOrNs1Rnd44
'Searchin', Hazel Dean, 1984　　　　youtu.be/w4bAt2wZXsU
'Catch Me'. Marsha Raven, 1983　　　youtu.be/y11B5XBD_iA
'Mourir sur scène', Dalida, 1983　　　youtu.be/NN2mxivM8Bo
'Gigi l'amoroso', Dalida, 1974　　　　youtu.be/BmHEkiJVs-g
'Non, je ne regrette rien', Edith Piaf, 1960
　　　　　　　　　　　　　　　　　youtu.be/Q3Kvu6Kgp88
'Big in Japan', Alphaville, 1984　　　youtu.be/tl6u2NASUzU

Lost Places
Stephanie Dickinson

We mourn their loss

The lost places

The memories

The people we met there

Friends made

Lives shared

Lovers found

… and lost

Safe places

When the world was not

The lost places

Gone …

But always there

Authors' Biographies

STEPHANIE DICKINSON trained as a primary school teacher in her thirties, and that job, and her children, took all her time and energy! Now retired she has the time and opportunity to develop a range of diverse interests. These include writing; working as a voluntary woodland ranger; photography; walking, especially with her dog, and volunteering at the London Metropolitan Archive.

JOHN DIXON has published two volumes of short stories, *The Carrier Bag* and *Whispering Campaigns,* and a volume of poems, *Seeking, Finding, Losing*. He hopes to publish his diary extracts shortly, as well as a novel *Push harder, Mummy, I want to Come Out*.

JEFFREY DOORN was born in New Jersey and now lives with his civil partner in South London. His work has appeared in *Gawp and Gaze*, *Queer Haunts*, *People Your Mother Warned You About*, *The Best of Gazebo*, *A Boxful of Ideas* (which he co-edited) and local history publications. He contributed to and co-edited poetry anthologies *Slivers of Silver*, *Oysters and Pearls* and *Coming Clean*.

DAVID DOWNING founded the Highlands and Islands' first LGBT+ magazine, *UnDividingLines*[1] in 2014, and his articles and fiction have appeared in a wide variety of publications, including *People Your Mother Warned You About* (Paradise Press) and *Out There* (Freight Books). He lives in the northwest Highlands.

DAVID FLYBURY was born in Ipswich in 1963, moved to London in 1984, met his husband in 1997, married in 2021. His novel *The Dalliance*, and short stories, *Fragmentarium*, deal with growing up, coming out, relationships, death, travel, Art and history ... and a few other things. Oh, and sex.

---

[1] www.undividinglines.wordpress.com

JILL GARDINER was a social historian and poet. She first discovered lesbian oral history when she joined Brighton Ourstory Project, and was one of the editors of their pioneering book *Daring Hearts: Lesbian and Gay Lives in 50s and 60s Brighton* (QueenSpark, 1992). Among the interviewees were women whose memories inspired her book *From the Closet to the Screen: Women at the Gateways Club 1945–85* (Pandora, 2003), which was described as 'fascinating and sometimes hilarious' by *The Observer*. Also a poet, her collection *With Some Wild Woman: Poems 1989–2019* was published by Tollington Press in 2019.

> Sadly, Jill died 29 March 2023, as this book was in production. A great loss – ed.

ZEKRIA IBRAHIMI writes: My sad life has been a nasty non-event on the way to death. I am a pensioner, aged 64, who has contributed only his own mental illness to those around him. Should I regret my emotional ugliness? My incapacity for love? Yes, I am afraid …

V. G. LEE is the author of five novels and two collections of short stories. Her most recent novel, *Mr Oliver's Object of Desire* was runner up for the YLVA Publishing Literary Prize for Fiction 2017 and she was long-listed for the BBC National Short Story Award 2022. She is also a judge for the Polari Book Prize.

ELIZABETH JANET LISTER, Beth, born 1934. Bright, sensitive, obedient, abused. Successful book-learning hid her non-value of self. Marriage and two daughters, divorce at 36. Help from MIND at 50 and realises she's bisexual, a painter, a writer, a knitter, a gardener. Lives in Scotland near her daughters.

GARY MCGHEE is a semi-retired screenwriter, loving the outdoor life with his partner in the Norfolk countryside. Gary was 'red-pilled' before it became fashionable, and believes in liberty, freedom, modernism, and defying herd-mentalities. His novel *Andromono* was published in 2022.

ADRIAN RISDON'S heyday was in the 1970s, when he directed Antony Gormley in verse-drama, drank with Peter Ackroyd and commenced his role of amanuensis to the blind poet John Heath-Stubbs. From 1980 onward, however, Adrian's luck changed. He now lives in an Almshouse of Noble Poverty in Winchester.

PETER SCOTT-PRESLAND is founder/director of Homo Promos Theatre Company, and has been writer, performer and activist for over 50 years. He is the author of *Amiable Warriors: A Space to Breathe*, part one of a trilogy about the history of CHE published by Paradise Press, and two volumes of 'unreliable vignettes' entitled *A Gay Century*. All three are available in the Homo Promos shop.[2]

IAN TOWNSON has been involved in LGBT+ politics for the past 49 years. He started as a gay troublemaker in 1974, taking part in 'zapping' a conference on Psycho-Sexual disorders by distinguished psychiatrists and medical professionals pontificating on homosexuality and what to do about it. Escaping to London in October that year he became involved in the first ever gay community centre, squatted and established, in Brixton. The centre ran many activities and campaigns, becoming a focal point to draw more gay men into the area; eventually ten houses were squatted back-to-back on Mayall and Railton Roads with a shared garden in between. The squats became part of Brixton Housing Cooperative and are still there today. Ian is currently involved in Queer Wandsworth and the Rainbow Plaque Project.

LEIGH V. TWERSKY lives in London, where he was born. While he has had short stories and poems published before, he is delighted to have non-fiction work included in this anthology. He is currently looking forward to the publication of a gay-themed novel set in a dystopian Britain.

---

[2] www.homopromos.org/shopping.html